Praise for
Leadership Beyond Reason

"John takes the leader to a new level of performance by demonstrating there is more to leadership than traditional thinking would suggest. John's principles take you beyond reason, but they work; apply them, and you will become a more impactful and fulfilled leader."

—GREG CAMPBELL, former executive vice president, Coldwell Banker

"Learning what motivates your leadership decisions 'beyond reason' will help you make the good ones and, just as important, avoid the bad ones. This book is an intriguing and thought provoking analysis of effective leadership."

—GARY DAICHENDT, former executive vice president for worldwide operations, Cisco Systems

"Just another leadership book? *Not hardly!* John Townsend challenges us to look beyond the usual sources as we develop *leadership skill.* Values, feelings, and intuition are key tools in producing exceptional leaders. John presents a compelling case for going 'beyond reason' to acquire all the essential components of a good leader. His thorough assessment of the importance of values, thoughts, emotions, relationships, and transformation is productive and thought provoking. Why would we settle for anything less than a complete toolbox?"

—BILL YINGLING, former chairman and CEO, Thrifty Corp.

"Dr. John Townsend's new book, *Leadership Beyond Reason,* debuts at the perfect moment, amidst the bedlam of our turbulent times. It presents a magnificent challenge to both seasoned and aspiring leaders to approach leadership from a fresh and redemptive perspective, pivoting on the too long glossed over intangibles—values, thoughts, emotions, and relationships."

—ALLAN O. HUNTER JR., cofounder, Rent.com

"John reminds us we are in the *people* business. Many in leadership roles tend to ignore their emotions or assume their influence is negative and a threat to their effectiveness. John presents a compelling case for learning to recognize, integrate, and leverage our emotions for greater leadership results."

—FRED GLADNEY, owner, Trinity Consulting; and former director and general manager of services, Compaq

---

The material from this book is an essential part of Dr. Townsend's personal Leadership Coaching Program for executives, small business owners, and managers. Read what the participants of the program say about their experiences and how these principles have changed their approaches to leadership.

"The Leadership Coaching Program has helped me grow emotionally and professionally in ways that have produced measurable results in both arenas."

—TONY DAUS, executive vice president, AMEC (FTSE 100 company)

"The interaction is personal, and I can see amazing changes that I believe are actual and permanent, both in my work life and personal life."

—JOHN TIBBITS, former owner, Inline Corporation

"As a leader, I get to learn and grow, being sharpened by the group. I gain insight into myself and others that will benefit me forever as I aim to build relationships and be an influencer."

—GLENN HANSEN, former district manager, Best Buy

"I am noticing significant improvements in how I am operating my company and in the results I am experiencing. Dr. Townsend's personal involvement, the team's interaction, and the homework assignments, over time, have been key for me."

—DAN BERGMANN, president, Interstate Gas Services

Leadership Beyond Reason

Other Books by Dr. John Townsend

Boundaries

It's Not My Fault

Who's Pushing Your Buttons?

Handling Difficult People

How to Have that Difficult Conversation You've Been Avoiding

Leadership
Beyond
Reason

How Great Leaders Succeed by Harnessing
the Power of Their Values, Feelings, and Intuition

Dr. John Townsend

THOMAS NELSON
Since 1798

NASHVILLE   DALLAS   MEXICO CITY   RIO DE JANEIRO   BEIJING

Published in Nashville, Tennessee, by Thomas Nelson. Thomas Nelson is a registered trademark of Thomas Nelson, Inc.

Published in association with Yates & Yates, LLP, www.yates2.com.

Thomas Nelson, Inc. titles may be purchased in bulk for educational, business, fund-raising, or sales promotional use. For information, please e-mail SpecialMarkets@ThomasNelson.com.

All Scripture quotations are taken from New American Standard Bible®, © The Lockman Foundation 1960, 1962, 1963, 1968, 1971, 1972, 1973, 1975, 1977, 1995. Used by permission.

Some names and identifying details have been changed to protect the identities of those involved.

Library of Congress Cataloging-in-Publication Data

Townsend, John Sims, 1952–
 Leadership beyond reason : how great leaders succeed by harnessing the power of their values, feelings, and intuition / John Townsend.
   p. cm.
 Includes bibliographical references.
 ISBN 978-0-7852-2877-6 (hardcover)
 1. Leadership—Religious aspects—Christianity. 2. Leadership—Moral and ethical aspects. 3. Values. 4. Character. I. Title.
 BV4597.53.L43T69 2009
 253—dc22   2008042161

Printed in the United States of America

09 10 11 12 13 QW 5 4 3

To those who undertake the role of leadership
with all your heart, soul, strength, and mind.

And to my father.
You led your family and your business in the right paths.
Thank you for being an example of leadership for me.

CONTENTS

ACKNOWLEDGMENTS

Thanks to the following people who helped, in many ways, to bring about this book:

The leaders and organizations I have worked with over the years. I have so appreciated your dedication to your missions and your ability to persevere and succeed.

Sealy Yates and Jeana Ledbetter. As my literary agents, you helped create the *big picture* of a leadership book that dealt with the internal world and partnered with me in its formation. Thanks for your help in pushing the envelope.

Mike Hyatt, president and CEO of Thomas Nelson, Inc. Your concept of the heart in leadership has been valuable to me, as has your encouragement on this material.

Joey Paul. You kept up the original excitement and vision of these ideas. Your own life and career are examples of the theme of this book.

Acknowledgments

Jennifer Stair, the copy editor who helped shape the manuscript. Your craft and care for how the ideas are presented have made this a much more engaging book.

Keith Hammer, who provided the title for this book. You epitomize how creativity and diligence can go hand in hand.

Bill Butterworth, Gary Daichendt, Roy Englebrecht, Jim Franklin, Frank Foster, Fred Gladney, Eric Heard, John Higman, Allan Hunter, Jerry Pharris, and Bill Yingling. Your lives, character, and leadership are a continuing example to me of how it's done the right way. Thank you for walking through life with me.

Members of the Leadership Coaching Program, Blue and Red Teams. Your dedication to the twin processes of personal growth and leadership development are ongoing inspirations for me.

Dr. Howard Hendricks. Your pioneering work in the value and development of leadership has transformed generations. Thank you for your personal time and tutelage with me.

Maureen Price, who directs the Ultimate Leadership Workshop. You continually shepherd and improve the workshop in ways that create growth and change for so many leaders.

Bill Dallas, CEO of Church Communication Network. Your partnership in helping make leadership training accessible in so many venues is making a significant difference in the world.

Dr. Henry Cloud. It has been a great experience conceptualizing and working on the issues of leadership and the psychological world. Thank you for who you are as a person and as a friend.

INTRODUCTION

J eff said to us, "I'm afraid."

We paid attention. *Afraid* isn't a word you normally hear from successful businessmen and leaders. I would have expected *concerned*, *wary*, or *hesitant*, but not a word describing the emotion of fear.

Jeff was discussing work issues with several other executives and business owners, and he had brought up a prospective deal he was considering with another company. It was a significant growth opportunity, yet there was serious risk involved. He bounced the idea off us, and we were asking questions and giving feedback. In the midst of our discussion of numbers issues, strategic concerns, logistical matters, and values considerations, Jeff said, matter-of-factly, "I'm afraid." He then went on to tell us about the downsides he was concerned about. There were several, including the current economy's effect on his business, cash flow concerns, and whether or not the other company's culture was the right fit for his own. These were matters that would make anyone afraid, concerned, wary, or hesitant. They were not necessarily deal breakers; they were more like warning flags. So we were surprised to hear Jeff saying that he was *afraid*. It seemed unusual.

A few days later, I talked to Jeff. He told me he had decided against the deal. When I asked him why, his reasons had to do both with the numbers and with his internal anxiety. Both parts corresponded. And both his reasons and his intuition helped him sleep better at night, knowing he had made the right decision.

> Great leaders succeed by harnessing
> the power of both the external world
> and the internal world.

This conversation remained with me because it illustrated something significant about leadership. Jeff paid attention to two worlds of information available to him: the world of objective reality and the world of subjective response. Of hard data and soft data. Ultimately, of his *external world* and his *internal world*. One did not have precedence over the other. In our conversation, both worlds advanced and retreated as we discussed different aspects of his situation. Both the data and Jeff's internal response had value and were relevant to the decision he faced.

And that, quite simply, is the premise of this book. Great leaders succeed by harnessing the power of both the external world and the internal world. You, as a leader, are probably more trained, prepared, and experienced in the external world than you are in the inner one. Most likely, you are able to amass large amounts of valuable information from reports, research, journals, and interviews. And you need that information; it is critical to your success as a leader. At the same time, you also need access to data within you that is just as valuable and helpful to how you lead, come to conclusions, and make decisions.

This book is designed to help you understand what is inside you—what is "beyond reason"—and how to use that to help you succeed. Reason, in the sense of using rationality, logic, and objective sources of information, is clearly a necessary core component of leadership. No person of influence can function at high levels without it. However, there are also important leadership aspects that are beyond, or in addition to, pure reasoning. They are more subjective, internal, and experiential. These *beyond reason* aspects are not infallible, but they are highly significant and valuable. The complete leader, who wants to be empowered for the next level, must know how to operate with all the possible tools. This is what separates the great leaders from the good ones.

> This book is designed to help you understand what is inside you—what is "beyond reason"—and how to use that to help you succeed.

There are several ways to describe what is beyond pure reason alone. Sometimes it is called your subjective, internal, or inner world. However, at the end of the day, it is simply *your immaterial life*. Within you are passions, values, feelings, and intuitions, as well as thoughts. They cannot be seen or touched because they are not physical. But they are real, they exist, they are an essential part of you, and they will do well for you.

In this book, I describe several key aspects of your inner world, what they do, and how you—the leader—can use them to bring the results you want and need to bring. Don't be put off by the psychobabble sound of the terms. These internal aspects of who you are will, if used in the right way, be a sound part of your leadership repertoire.

Where Are You?

Here are a few introductory questions that will help you gain a better understanding of where you are in this dimension of your leadership:

- In the leadership training you have received, how much emphasis was placed on the value of your own subjective and personal experience?

- Have you ever made a *gut* leadership decision that did not seem to be logical but ultimately proved to be successful?

- Conversely, have you ever ignored your gut and realized later that it was a mistake to do that?

- Has your own experience with emotions in leadership indicated to you that feelings are a help or a hindrance to you reaching your goals?

- Do those in your leadership environment tend to trust objective information over internal information?

- If you were asked to describe how you use your inner self to lead, how clearly would you be able to explain it?

- When you are under pressure to produce results, do you tend to rely on hard facts and dismiss the subjective elements?

If your responses to these questions landed on the objective side of things, that is normal for most leaders. There are good reasons for this. You have a responsibility to create good outcomes and to help people achieve them. The outcomes are generally measurable, such as profits, stock value, or some growth metric. Because leaders are evaluated in objective and measurable ways, you may tend to look only at the facts to help you achieve your goals.

The process is similar to the outcome, in that sense. You trust what you see and read, things that can be proven and measured. For example, a profit-and-loss statement is reliable. It has the facts. The information is there, in black and white, and it does not change. It is hard data. However, *you ignore what is beyond reason to your peril.* As we will see in this book, leaders who don't pay attention to the subjective will miss a great deal of importance, ranging from an emotional response like Jeff's fear, to the ability to relate to and understand those you work with and lead. Missing this information can affect the quality of your judgments and decisions.

You ignore what is beyond reason to your peril.

There is another reason most leaders answer the above questions on the objective side, and it is the belief that the subjective world slows down your edge, gets you off focus, or makes you become too touchy-feely. You become concerned that *inner* matters will distract you from your goals and mission. You begin to think that too much introspection will make you less decisive. There is logic to this thinking, actually. If you, the leader, are to run ahead of your competition, doesn't the process of stopping to see what you feel, sense, believe, or think slow things down? In the short term, certainly. Paying attention to your inside world takes some amount of time. But in the long term, learning to deal with your insides brings a high return on investment. That is one reason for the popularity of leadership books on values, emotional intelligence,[1] and personal growth. The internal supports the external—and it produces results.

Scan Your Inner World

The simplest way to understand how you can use your inner world, the world beyond reason, is to look at it in the same way you look at how you get information from external sources. Most leaders regularly read the newspaper or get the news online or on TV. You subscribe to magazines and journals in your area of specialty. You receive reports and e-mails on your organizations. Leaders are information junkies, and they need to be. You are constantly scanning the horizon to look at trends, the future, opportunities, threats, and people. Similarly, you also need to be able to do an *interior scan*—that is, you need the skill to access what's going on inside you, regularly and on demand, so you can tap into that source as well. One of the major goals of this book is to help you hone the ability of scanning the different aspects of your inner world. The more information you have about your inner world, generally the better you can decide and lead.

You need the skill to access what's going on
inside you, regularly and on demand,
so that you can tap into that source.

Not only that but those you lead also have an inner world, a subjective experience. They have feelings, creativity, and their own thoughts. Their lives also have areas that are beyond reason. As a leader, you must connect with their insides, to develop them as people and producers. This cannot be done if you are not in the process yourself. All of us have had the experience of being led by someone who may have been competent and principled but was simply clueless about subjective matters. You may have respected and liked the person, but you probably also found that he could not understand nuances of what you were trying to say, or differences you had, or your emotional experiences. And this lack of understanding was probably more than frustrating; it likely didn't move the mission of the organization along. Leaders who can understand their own fears, as Jeff did, are better able to understand the fears of those they lead. As you scan your inner world, you help others scan theirs as well.

Not a 180 but an Addition

If you regularly read books on leadership and business, you are probably aware that there is a tendency for an author to present his approach as a new paradigm that revolutionizes everything that has come before, so the new book will be a 180-degree change in direction for the leader and the organization. That is not the case for this book.

Though there are classics in leadership literature, must-reads for any leader, I shy away from 180-degree proclamations. Leadership has been studied and researched by many competent people for many years. I think most leadership books that make substantial contributions build on what has already been done well. They add to the leader's repertoire of abilities and skills. They remove some unhelpful ways of thinking, conceptualizing, relating, and behaving. But they don't remove the good stuff.

I want you to continue your own leadership training in this very significant aspect of the inner world and its contents. The principles described here are compatible with sound leadership theories and practices that already work for you. So look at this book as helping you to achieve great results by going deeper into what is already inside you.

Though my primary focus in this book is harnessing the power of leadership beyond reason, I will not ignore reason. Because of the importance of reason in successful leadership, chapter 2 will explain how leaders can improve and better utilize their thoughts and the thinking process.

Who Are You?

Let's clarify who this book is for, as *leader* is a broad term. Basically, this material is designed for you if you are engaged in *influencing others to achieve results and goals*. To influence someone is to have an effect on them. To make a difference. Much has been written on the power of influence, and this gives room for all sorts of people to qualify as leaders. Here are some examples:

- Corporate executives and managers

- Small business owners
- Physicians and those in the medical field
- Psychologists and those in the helping professions
- Pastors and ministry leaders
- Small group leaders and facilitators
- Teachers

It is a broad net. Effective leadership creates a setting in which people live better and are more productive, effective, creative, resourceful, and higher-functioning. More than that, leaders make their organization one with better results.

Where It All Began

You most likely became a leader for some reason that was beyond reason. Most of us don't start out in life thinking, *I don't know what I want to be good at, but I want to lead some people.* In fact, that could be an indication of a psychological problem. It's more likely that something inside you gradually came alive the more you grew, learned, and interacted with people. In other words, your inner world led you to leadership. For example:

- You liked working in teams and people told you, "You're good at motivating people."
- You had a vision to build an organization and realized you would need to recruit, train, and keep good people around you.
- You were an expert in some competency field and felt that it

wasn't enough, that you wanted to reach out and connect with others in addition to your expertise.

- You wanted to make a difference in some specific area of life or work, and you loved seeing people grow and change in that difference.

You probably would not have taken on the hard work, pressure, and demands of leadership had not your world beyond reason been moving and pushing you. It informs us, drives us, keeps us going in tough times, gives us wisdom and discernment, and connects us to others. It is often the part of us that first resonated with the possibility that we might be a good leader doing a worthwhile endeavor.

Keeping Your Eye on the Ball

I consulted many friends in business and leadership during the process of writing this book, and they have all said something like this: "Show the reader how harnessing the power of the inner world brings results." Leaders are under tremendous pressure to bring about outcomes and results. The bottom line belongs to the leader, whether it is revenues, profits, production, lives changed, or number of meetings. Any way you look at it, leaders must keep their eye on the ball.

Dealing with the subjective world has everything to do with producing good results. It is an essential aspect of your own success and your ability to help others succeed. This book is not some kind of exercise in self-actualization that we hope will one day make a difference. When you finish reading this book, my goal is for you to say, "I not only understand myself better, but I can also see leadership results from what I have learned."

Introduction

Whatever leadership niche you are in, from the corporate world to leading a small group, you will discover aspects of your interior world that will come to your aid. You were designed with both an external world and an inner world, and they work well together. Accessing both of these areas will take a little knowledge and a little work, but it will help you be the leader you want to be. So we will begin with the first and most foundational aspect of the inner world of the leader: your values.

Chapter One

VALUES

The Bedrock of Leadership

Veteran actor Christopher Walken was being interviewed by a group of reporters about his life and work. The setting, an auditorium, was simple. Walken sat on a chair on an empty stage. The reporters sat in the audience seats. They asked him questions, and he answered off the cuff.

After several queries about his work and life, one journalist asked, "When you die and go to heaven, what do you want God to say to you?"

Walken replied, "'You were right.'"

Walken's clever comment underscores two realities that are necessary to every leader:

1. *It is important to have values.*
2. *It is important to have the right values.*

I will add a third one to that, which we will examine later in this chapter:

3. *It is important for your values to be from inside you.*

Your leadership, as well as your life,
will reflect your values, for good or for bad.

Your values are beyond reason. That is, they are true and absolute for you, whether or not you think about them. Your values are simply aspects of reality that are guides for you. In Walken's case, "You were right" is another way of saying, "You lived life the right way. You were on the right path. You did life right. You oriented your moves so that the right things happened." That is what discovering your values is all about, thinking through the process of determining what guides and principles will order our steps. Values are about what is right and what matters.

Your inside life is the repository of your values, so we begin with values because most of your life springs from them. Your values are the bedrock of your identity. And your leadership, as well as your life, will reflect your values, for good or for bad. Some people are in prison right now because their values guided them to that end. And others are succeeding beyond their wildest dreams for the same reason.

What Are Values?

The word *value* basically means "worth." A value is something that you determine has a great deal of worth. So your values are those realities you believe in at the deepest level, so much so that they dictate your decisions and your leadership, even at your own risk.

The role of values in leadership and in the marketplace has received a great deal of attention and research for some time now.

Values

Experts today consider values to be critical to success.[1] Organizations spend a great deal of time working out the values that best fit their mission and context. Here are a few examples of values that leaders and organizations have used:

- Treating people well
- A quality product
- Customer service
- Innovation
- The best for less
- Excellence
- Making the organization a safe place for growth

The values of a group work best when they reflect the values of the leader. *Organizational values* help guide the mission, but *personal values* are ultimately where organizational values are derived from. As a leader, your personal values are about how you look at life, not just your organization. They are broader and more universal. They operate in business, in life, in love, in family. As you look at the examples below, you can see how personal values define the organizational ones:

- Love
- Caring for the welfare of others
- Truthfulness
- Allowing others choices
- Fairness

- Taking ownership
- Personal integrity
- A commitment to reality

I believe it's a mistake to come up with organizational values until you have done the work of determining your personal ones. Personal values will always override organizational values. For example, if a person does not have a high value for allowing choice and giving freedom to others (the micromanager scenario), it isn't likely that innovation will occur in the organization, as control hinders creativity. So the order is personal values first, organizational values second.

Wholehearted Values

Say, however, that you have spent time determining both your organizational and personal values. There is another step to consider here as well, and that is *whether or not your values are really and authentically from you.* How can you know if your stated values are ones that are actually part of who you are? I have seen many leaders who considered their organizational values in some sort of consultation or task setting and were diligent about it. And the result was a Word document, an e-mail, a poster, a reminder of things that everyone signed off on. But at the end of the day, no one would really and truly change their behavior based on these stated values. Nor would they think about them when faced with an opportunity or a problem. These values weren't part of the fabric of the leader's heart. They were helpful and potentially valuable, but they weren't considered.

For example, I was friends with a group of people in a corporation that provided media services. The CEO, Randy, was a very competent, creative, and positive person. He had come from another industry in the corporate environment and was adapting what he knew to the media world. One of Randy's strengths was that he didn't pretend to be perfect. He admitted when he was wrong, didn't hide mistakes, and was gracious when other people struggled. He talked about having a high value for authenticity, and people were drawn to his vulnerability. He laughed at his mistakes, and people in his organization felt safe and comfortable around him.

However, Randy didn't really play the tape all the way to the end in terms of what authenticity meant. When you have a high value for authenticity, it follows that you must also take responsibility for whatever you are being authentic about! So if you make a mistake and admit it, that is a good thing. But true authenticity means that you also do whatever you have to do to address and resolve the situation.

As it turns out, Randy made an error in judgment that cost the organization a great deal of money. He did not take into account some market shifts. That happens. It was a big deal but not so big that the organization wanted to let him go. They were willing to work with him, make the necessary corrections, and move on. Lesson learned. However, in order to do this, the board of directors began some very frank and direct talks with Randy so that everyone could do the right surgery, be on the same page, and resolve the issue.

It is important to make sure your values are wholehearted—that is, from the core of who you are.

After the second meeting, Randy resigned. He felt that the board was too harsh and unfair in their evaluations. I knew the board members and had heard their side of the situation. It sounded like while they were very honest, they were also on Randy's side and tried to be balanced. This was Randy's first serious mistake, and they were surprised by his reaction. With his previous *misdemeanor* offenses, Randy would admit his errors, people would be compassionate, and everyone would put them behind him. But this time, Randy's serious error in judgment was categorized a *felony* that could not be as easily overlooked. Due diligence and a lot of digging were necessary to do the job correctly.

Randy's resignation revealed that his value for authenticity was halfhearted. It looked good on paper and in small matters, but it wasn't real when it involved difficulty and confrontation. Randy was authentic to the point of admitting small problems; however, he did not have the stomach to look at his major failures. Instead, he felt misunderstood and persecuted when others pointed out serious problems even when they wanted to help him.

This is what I mean about your inner life. It is important to make sure your values are wholehearted—that is, from the core of who you are. How can you know? Here are some things to consider. Before you read the list of principles below, pull out your own list of values if you have one. With these stated values in mind, think about the principles below. This will help you see how deep down they go.

When Your Values Aren't Lived Out, It Bothers You

If your values are a part of you, you notice when they aren't fleshed out and executed, especially in a business or organization setting. Not only do you notice, but you are bothered by it. The event just doesn't register on your screen; you have an alert going off inside, saying, *This isn't OK with me!* You can't just pass it off.

For example, suppose fairness is one of your personal values; you want to see people treated justly in your group. Then say your direct report comes to you with a complaint about another individual and neglects to go to that person first. That is gossip. It hurts people, and it isn't fair treatment. If fairness is a deep value, you will be bothered by this even though the information about the individual could be useful to you. But the bigger picture is what you respond to, and your sense of being disturbed is a good thing.

When it comes to values, you want to always know who you are.

Before the national elections last year, I attended a fund-raiser. The speaker, a well-known leader, was talking about the upcoming presidential election, and he went over the positions the candidates were taking on various issues. Then he talked about the dilemma most of us face in an election: we don't agree with everything any one candidate says, so how do we decide for whom to vote? His values *aha* statement that stuck with me was, "There are some issues I don't have to agree with and will still vote for a candidate. But some issues are so important to me that if I voted for a person who disagreed with my position on them, *I wouldn't know who I am anymore.*" That is what I mean by "when your values aren't lived out, it bothers you." Compromise and negotiation are valuable in leadership. But when it comes to values, you want to always know who you are.

Some people can be faced with values dilemmas and not be bothered. They quickly make a decision, count the losses, and move on. This is not a good sign. It could mean that they haven't really delved into the value, and it's still an idea, but no more. Or it could mean that they think more in terms of what author James O'Toole calls *contingency*, meaning that the values aren't universal but relative to the situation.[2] These people believe they can change the rules of integrity if the situation warrants it, which is a serious problem. Finally, it could mean that they have a character problem, and instead of seeking consistency and integration inside, they compartmentalize incompatible realities. They aren't upset when values are violated. This requires more work if that is the case.

When Your Values Are Lived Out, You Know Why

This is the flip side of the previous principle. If your values are a part of you, you notice when they are being lived out. You see the value that undergirds the situation, and you understand why and how it operates.

Taking the example above, your direct report comes to you after he has done the hard work of confronting the individual. Unfortunately, the individual was defensive or nonresponsive. So now your direct report asks you for help with the individual, as you are his next step in the protocol. You know that it was difficult for him to attempt to talk to the individual. But he was being fair to the individual. It was the right thing to do. And you know it was not only the right thing for the organization, but it bodes well for your group's success. People do better when they know they are treated fairly. And people in your organization trust you and your best practices more because you play by the rules. So you see values executed, you understand why, and you know that, as my partner Dr. Henry Cloud says, "The good guys win."[3]

You Experience Your Values More than Memorizing Them

When your values are internally based, you often don't even think about them explicitly. They have become so ingrained that they are just part of how you think, judge, and lead. It's certainly helpful to review your list of values and continue updating and improving them. But when they are the right ones, it's more like you *live what you value.*

Here's a recent example of this. I was working with a pastor who had a rocky relationship with one of his colleagues. He had disagreed with a decision his colleague had made, and in response, the other pastor had accused him of victimizing him and began an informal underground campaign against the first pastor. The conflict was threatening to tear the church apart. People were taking sides. After carefully listening to information from both sides, I believed the first pastor was in the right and the second one was clearly wrong. I went to the first one and said, "I believe you in this situation. But I think you should call the other pastor and offer to reconcile somehow. I know he should call you first, but because he feels like you've treated him wrong, he won't. If you want to solve this problem, I think it's your move."

I knew that this pastor had a high value on ownership—that is, taking responsibility for his life and his outcomes. The man didn't hesitate. He immediately picked up the phone and made the call. He humbled himself to being the one who *owned* the problem and reached out to the other pastor though he had been wronged. The second man eventually left, but his exit was not nearly as traumatic to the church as it could have been.

I want to focus on the *immediate* part of this story. I had expected the first pastor to say something like, "It's *his* problem; why doesn't he come to me?" He could have, except that he was living out the ownership value. He did not have to pull out an index card with his list of values and review what he should do. There was no need to. His internal world had already been informed by his values, and he went the extra mile of ownership.

You Think About Values in Terms of Your Outcomes

Let's return to the big idea of this book: leading from your inner world ultimately produces better results in your leadership. So as you work on your organization, your people, and your goals, you are able to see how the right values are essential in bringing about the fruit you want. They are in your conversations, plans, and decisions. For example, I complimented a friend of mine who is part owner of a manufacturing organization. He had told me his story of how he had begun at nineteen with nothing, apprenticing himself to an older man. He had truly begun at the lowest rung of the ladder. Now, in his forties, he was quite successful.

Leading from your inner world ultimately produces better results in your leadership.

I was impressed by his work. When I complimented him, he said, "A lot of this is because I have tried to be aware that there's a lot I don't know, so I always need to listen and learn." As they say, he knows what he doesn't know. Not surprisingly, my friend has a high personal value of reality. He has no need to be seen as anyone special. He has a commitment to understand reality so that he can help his organization. And you can see that, in our conversation, his mind immediately went to his value on reality as soon as I complimented him. He tied in his good outcomes to his value, an indication that it goes deep inside him.

The Sources of Values

We all have values. Values are principles that are important to you. *Something* is important to you, so begin by figuring out what things matter to you.

Though you may have done values work already, it's important to unpack where your values come from. As you become aware of their origins, you will be better able to improve on and live out your values.

Values from the Inside

It is important to look inside yourself when it comes to establishing your values. You may find out a great deal about what is important to you, for good or for bad, by looking internally.

In Words. Sometimes, when I am training leaders, I ask them to write down their values. The usual flip chart method is fine for that; it is a very good launching point for a discussion on values. However, you generally tend to come up with ideas of what you'd *like to be* important, *want to be* important, or *think it would be a good idea to be* important. My experience is that if you stop here, you don't get a great deal of helpful information. It's generally a pretty idealistic list, and everyone signs off on it, but it just doesn't truly guide the life of the organization because it's not really from the inner world. You need the list of words, and it's good to begin with it, but you need more than the list. That is why I take things to another level, to help tease out what is really there.

In Behavior. Your actions, your history, and your behavior are the true gold mine for your values. You already dictate your steps according to some sort of guiding principles. It's the famous say-do issue. Saying is always trumped by doing. Our behavior tells us much more than our words, in terms of what we really believe.

In my experience, most leaders actually have some key values they have not only framed into words but also live out in their behavior. There is a consistency in how they lead, and their values matter to them. At the same time, however, most leaders have some other values that are running things, and these need to be looked at. These are values you may have no awareness of whatsoever, but they play a very important role in your life.

For example, I was training some small group leaders in how to be effective in helping their group members grow in the process. We were talking about values. I asked them to describe their last group session. One woman said, "I feel a little bad about this. I facilitate a couples' group, and we are studying a book about marriage and communication. Our last meeting, I didn't even get to the lesson for that night. I guess maybe I don't value learning enough."

"Maybe," I said. "But I don't think we know enough yet to make that call. Why didn't you get to the lesson?"

She said, "Well, as soon as we began, one of the members said she had been diagnosed with cancer that week, and she and her husband were overwhelmed. We spent the whole time, and late into the night, listening to them, supporting them, and praying for them."

I told her, "I don't think this is about a lack of value for learning. It's a very high value for compassion for people." She made the right call based on her care for her struggling friend. This decision was based on her value for the welfare of others. Whether or not she had written it down, her behavior described her value.

This approach can also unearth values you don't really want to have. That is, sometimes our behavior tells us things about ourselves that aren't very positive. However, if we are aware of these things, we can change them. If we aren't, we're stuck in a bad situation.

For example, a small business owner I worked with told me one of his stated values was honesty. He believed in truthfulness both in his business and in his personal life. And in most of the areas of his life, his saying and his doing were the same. He had a reputation of integrity with customers, vendors, and employees. However, there was a problem area: he had some severe conflicts with his business partner. The partner was a charming and personable man, but he was, to be blunt, a slacker. He didn't bring in a lot of business, nor did he take the reins in running the company. He made some contributions, but not nearly at the 50 percent partner rate.

Sometimes our behavior tells us things about ourselves that aren't very positive. However, if we are aware of these things, we can change them.

As I got to know the structure and the finances of the company, it became very apparent that my client was carrying much more weight than he should. When I asked him about it, he brushed it off, saying, "It's more of an intangible. He's a really good guy." But as I continued discussing this issue with him, he finally admitted that he knew it was true, and he resented the inequity.

The payoff came when I asked him, "Do you want to talk to your partner about it?"

His face reddened, and his hands started shaking. "I just could never do that," he said. "I've tried to talk to him about similar situations, and it blew up in my face. It was a nightmare. I just don't do that well with confrontation. I'm more of a lover than a fighter, I guess."

I began to understand and felt a great deal of compassion for the man. He was in a bind. So I phrased the issue in terms of values. I said, "Then maybe it's fair to say that your value for honesty is sometimes trumped by a value for keeping the peace." You could see the lightbulb going on in his head as he thought about it. He'd never realized that his fear of conflict, especially with his partner, was emerging as a guiding value—but one that was guiding him in the wrong way. He began to understand that, though it had never entered his mind, his anxiety about confrontation led to a negative value that limited his success.

Fortunately, that realization motivated him to work on his problems in confronting people. In time, he became more comfortable and skilled in resolving conflict, and he ultimately had *the talk* with the partner. The partner didn't take it well, and eventually the business split. Though it was a difficult time for my client, within a year he was more successful as a sole proprietor than he had been in the partnership, and things have gotten even better over the years. This was no mystery, for he was the driving force of the business. The real mystery, that of a harmful value, had been solved, and he was able to move on.

Negative Values to Resolve. Here are a few more examples from the *dark* side for you to consider in your own leadership. Though it may not be a positive experience for you, identifying any potential negative values may help you to prevent some catastrophes or, as in the above example, set a new and better direction for your organization.

- *Being perceived by others as a good person.* Some leaders want to prevent others from seeing them as imperfect, being wrong, or having a bad attitude. This can result in endless explanations as to why the leader did what he did, rather than the leader explaining himself as well as he can and then letting those people who need to be upset with him simply be upset with him.

- *Focusing on results to the detriment of people.* Some leaders find themselves in the classic leadership bind of running over people's feelings in order to achieve an objective. Most leaders who do this aren't aware of it. They see this value as a "passion for excellence," and people's hurts are interpreted as overreactions. Leaders with this negative value often need others helping them evaluate behaviors from a more objective vantage point.

- *Having it all together.* Some leaders tend not to admit problems, even though they are really struggling. With this value, the leader often is on the way to some sort of failure or breakdown. There is generally a fear that others will be critical or judgmental, which keeps up the pressure to have it all together.

- *Dismissing the negative so that it is spun as positive.* This describes the leader who, when faced with a problem, is not willing to admit how serious it might be, whether it is about finances, personnel, marketing, or other leadership. He values being positive to the point that he loses touch with reality. People become discouraged with this sort of leader and eventually stop bringing problems to him, as they know he won't listen to how they really feel.

Consider these values, and then address the negative values that are hindering your growth and leadership. Most of them, at the deepest level, are about fear. Face the fears, get a few people around who care about you, and talk about your fears. You will find that you operate on better values the more you experience, discuss, and take risks with these problem values. Becoming aware of them is often the hardest part.

Anything that is important to your inner world is best deposited there through personal and real experience. So the more you discuss these negative values, analyze them, open them up to the scrutiny of others, make decisions based on them, make mistakes and correct yourself, fine-tune them, or even throw some out, it all helps. They become part of your heart, and they eventually drive your best decisions.

Values from the Outside

In addition to looking inside yourself, you can add values from other sources that are wonderful leadership principles. None of us is finished yet in life; hopefully we are always open to finding new ideas that can help us change, inspire people, and create good results in our endeavors.

Those You Trust. It's a good idea to talk to leaders you know and ask them about their own values: what they are, how they crafted them, which ones are the most important. If these leaders are doing a good job and are friends of yours, it's likely they will not only be somewhat like-minded, but they may also add a value you haven't considered, one that would work well with you. For example, I have a friend in the corporate world who reads a great deal of leadership literature. He often mentions something he's learned from an article or writer. He told me one day that he tries to be the kind of leader people aren't afraid of—except for the fear of letting the team down. I had not thought of that, but it made sense to me, and I worked it into my own set of values.

Leaders in History. I benefit a great deal from reading or listening to podcasts concerning the thoughts and lives of great leaders in history. Most leaders are time-starved, and it's sometimes difficult to see this as a priority. But I recommend that you carve out a few minutes or a few hours a week, on a regular basis, to learn from what other leaders have done before you. For example, something Mother Teresa said meant a great deal to me: "Do not wait for leaders. Do it alone, person to person." In my own life and leadership, that speaks to two values: (1) taking initiative, rather than waiting for a rescuer; and (2) being connected to others face-to-face, in little ways, as an avenue to getting larger matters accomplished.

Spiritual Truths. The spiritual realities of life are another source of values. Transcendent truths about what matters and what is ultimately important are central to many leaders' perspectives of leadership, relationship, and organizations. For example, the book of Proverbs in the Bible is a profound source of leadership values. We will deal with spirituality in more depth in chapter 5.

Reading this section may cause you to think, *How can something I get from the outside be a part of my own internal life?* It is true that these external sources may end up in a notebook on a shelf. But sometimes there is a dynamic interchange between the truth you just read and your own life. It's a resonance; you experience its reality at a deep level inside. Your inner world isn't a vacuum, waiting to be filled with values. It is not passive and empty. It is active thinking and feeling. It is evaluating. It is watching and observing what you watch and observe. So when you encounter a value that makes sense to you, *the external value gives structure and words to something already inside yourself.* For example, I read that quote from Mother Teresa and said to myself, *I would never have thought of it that way, but she said what I believe.*

As you can see, then, as you identify and develop your values, you need both the inside and the outside. We need to constantly be on the prowl for good leaders who have good values. And we need to expose their thoughts to our own subjective worlds and see what happens. Good people are good for good people.

What Now?

Think about your *blue sky* values, the darker values you need to resolve and the external values you appreciate and want to adopt. Make them part of your mission and your practice. You don't need many of them. In fact, trying to keep up with too many stated values can be burdensome and you'll simply get discouraged and stop thinking about them. Like the popular elevator conversation concept, hone your values down to a list you can tell someone quickly and succinctly.

More importantly, don't forget the experience aspect of values. If your values aren't sufficiently internalized, over time they will lose power and meaning. It is much better to lose money or make a bad decision based on what you thought were the right values, than to make decisions that looked OK but were not made by consulting your values. The first is preferable because you will learn about your own leadership and how you make decisions. Or you may find that your values need revising. But at least you will be constructing a path to success that will last a lifetime and will help you continually improve. The other way, making decisions by the seat of your pants, gives you nothing to learn if things blow up. You don't know what you did wrong or what you can change. Values make the difference—if you let values be part of your experience and, in that process, part of your inner world.

Hone your values down to a list you can tell someone quickly and succinctly.

Another aspect of values is that, in the best scenarios, your values are integrated with the other parts of your subjective life. Your inner world contains not only values, but also thoughts, emotions, relationships, and transformation. These do not function well independently. They best operate together in a supportive and seamless fashion. So make sure you've thought through your values, just as you should with the other four leadership aspects we will deal with in this book, *especially in relation to these other parts.*

Here's an example. Say you want to incorporate the value of personal integrity; your organization does not tolerate deception or unethical practices. That is a sound value. Now look at this value in the following terms:

- *Thoughts.* Scour this value; discuss it and analyze it.

- *Emotions.* Does this value generate anxiety? Do you feel encouraged by this value; is it a good addition? Does it make you feel you will have to confront something in your company that needs to be confronted as a result?

- *Relationships.* Consider those who matter to you. What will their reactions be to this value? How will this value affect their lives?

- *Transformation.* Are you continuing to explore the meaning of this value? Are you more ethical today than you were a year ago?

These questions are valuable fodder for you as a growing, improving, and changing leader. Work with your values and with all these aspects of your heart, developing them into something that meshes, succeeds, and brings results.

Having laid this groundwork, let's now move to the part of the inner life that leaders often feel the most confidence in: your thoughts. Hopefully, you will learn some helpful things about how you think that can increase your leadership abilities.

Chapter Two

THOUGHTS

Leaders Think About Thinking

A longtime friend of mine, Jim, is a leader in his field, which has to do with the media industry. He is well respected for his insights, ethics, and the results he creates. I have had many conversations with Jim and have benefited from our friendship.

There is a pattern I have noticed with Jim and other effective leaders that goes like this. You present some knotty problem to him—for example, one with complexities in finances, people's personalities, market economies, and so on. You describe the situation to him from all the angles you can. You tell him where you're landing on it. You tell him what other people have said so far. And you say, "So what do you think? Do I fish or cut bait on this situation?"

Having listened carefully and having asked several good questions, Jim will be silent for a moment. Then he will say, "Let me get back to you."

It can be frustrating at the time. You've spent all this energy dissecting the situation, and now you have to wait. But having gone through this experience many times with Jim, I have found that the wait is worth it. He will call me in a few days and give me some perspective I hadn't thought of, and it will generally be very helpful.

Here is the point: not only had I not thought of the new perspective, but *neither had Jim, at the time.* When I first presented the situation to him, he really didn't know what he thought yet. Jim wasn't putting me off as some sort of lesson in learning patience. He really hadn't yet formulated his final opinion. He was actively listening and learning. Certainly he had ideas and options running around in his head when I told him my situation. Most of us do. But he knew that was not the right time for him to think. He wanted to take in everything he could and then spend some time ruminating on it all.

This approach works well. This doesn't mean, of course, that friends and advisers who give you answers on the spot can't provide great wisdom. Certainly they can and do. But the Jims of the world have a high batting average. They *think*, and they respect the time it takes to think well and in a thorough manner.

Not only that but the people whom Jim leads often feel the same way I do. The fact that he takes the time to think through their words and problems makes his answers significant and weighty to them. Those he leads and influences find this a major reason they follow him.

Your Heart Has a Brain

Like Jim, good leaders place a high value on thinking clearly and well. Most spend a great deal of time thinking, in all sorts of contexts. Sometimes it is alone in a room, reflecting. Sometimes it is in a decision-making meeting with colleagues. Sometimes it is an instant, under-the-gun process that moves very quickly. But thinking is critical.

Thinking is an internal activity. When you consider if one of your direct reports is in the right place for her talents, you are thinking. When you shift resources to a different area in the marketplace, that is thinking as well. When you consider what study materials to use with your small group in the next quarter, that is thinking. Just as with your values, your thoughts are part of what it takes to be a leader who looks inside and finds many things he needs in order to achieve the best results.

Good leaders place a high value on thinking clearly and well.

As I mentioned earlier, thinking—the reasoning part of your life and leadership—is critical and central to your work. That is why beyond reason also includes reason. Remember also that you learn about your mind by using your mind. The apparatus you are working with is also what you are observing. The apparatus you are observing is also the apparatus you are observing it with! I say this not as a matter of trivia but because I want you to be aware that your thoughts aren't always the right thoughts because your mind is fallible. I see too many leaders who never question their thoughts or their mental tendencies and quirks, and their leadership suffers. So be aware that your mind can make mistakes. The more you know about your thinking patterns, the better equipped you are for leadership.

Thinking . . . is critical and central to your work. That is why beyond reason also includes reason.

Thinking 101

As a leader, it's important for you to understand the basics of how you think, in order to think more effectively. The simplest definition of *thought* is an idea in the mind. In other words, a thought is some solution, brainstorm, strategy, insight, or observation. It can be about anything, but in the context of leadership, we're generally referring to thoughts about people, opportunities, and problems, the things you need to concentrate on.

A helpful way to look at thoughts is to contrast them to reactions. When you react to a situation, you don't act freely and independently. You make decisions based instead on internal factors such as fear, old habits, or people's opinions. Reactions can be devastating to a leader, and can shortchange his impact. Thinking, however, looks at alternatives, weighs consequences, considers costs and benefits, and uses judgment. Certainly thinking can be taken to the extreme, as when hard-charging business types critique the academic world about the "paralysis of analysis." But in the main, those who think thoroughly tend to make better decisions and tend to treat people in a way that makes them want to follow them.

I consulted with the CEO of a service organization who, in many respects, was a brilliant man. He had an incredible memory and understood financial complexities very well. However, he tended to have the same answer for every significant problem, and it was the old engineer's solution: If it doesn't work, use a hammer. If that doesn't work, use a bigger hammer.

For this CEO, the hammers were always the same: tighten down on expenses and work harder. There was nothing wrong with that, but that didn't solve all the major problems the company had. They needed new and different ideas. They needed *thoughts*. But his ideas were basically reactions to what had always worked for him in the past. Eventually, he and the company had to part ways because he was not providing the thinking that would have helped him. The sad thing is I think he could have had the right thoughts since he certainly had the capacity. But I don't think he was very interested or curious about his thinker.

You want to pay attention to keeping your mind in shape. There is a growing body of research that is beginning to indicate that as we age, we "use it or lose it" with our minds, especially in memory, vocabulary, and mathematics. Even if you don't retain the mental abilities, you may be able to keep sharper during the time you exercise your brain. For example, several times a week, I try to work out with an electronic game gadget designed to improve mental functioning. My teenage kids give me a hard time about not playing more fun games with the gadget, but it's no game to me. I want as much mind as I can have for as long as I can have it.

The Ways You Think

There are several dimensions to how successful leaders think that are important to know, to be aware of for yourself, and to develop.

Cognitive Style

Your cognitive style refers to the way you process information from your environment. It has to do with how you read journal articles, how you listen to what others tell you, and how you draw conclusions based on how you observe the workplace. There is a great deal of helpful research on this, including with leaders. One aspect of cognitive style I want to emphasize for this book is the *linear versus nonlinear style*.

Linear thinkers are more logical and ordered in how they think, while nonlinears come at problems and opportunities from different angles. Linear thinkers see a step-by-step approach to their work. Nonlinears try to see if there is a new way to look at an issue. This description is a broad one. People who research these matters disagree on what specific terms and descriptions to use, but for the purposes of this book, these distinctions describe the difference.

These styles have stereotypes associated with them. Managers and accountants are often seen as linear. Their tasks involve numbers, finances, budgets, schedules, quotas, and planning. Marketing and public relations types tend to be seen as nonlinear, with new ideas, promotions, analyzing the competition, keeping the attention of the consumer, and so forth. There certainly seems to be some reality to these stereotypes. However, there are two problems people commonly encounter with cognitive-style thinking. First, they tend to pigeonhole individuals into one style, and that can limit potential. Certainly we have our dominant cognitive style that we need to work from. But most people aren't totally one or the other. You can be involved in both.

For example, I know a woman who directs a small business in the communications industry, a sector in which there have been lots of changes over the years. She has had to wear many different hats in the company because of its size. The business wasn't large enough to hire full-time people for every type of role, so she had to learn to do some of the work herself.

While you have a primary cognitive style, don't limit yourself.

Her background was as a vice president in the larger corporate world, where she ran a division and established policies that were essentially linear tasks. In the new position, however, she found that she needed someone to write marketing copy that was interesting and presented the new company's products well—nonlinear type of work. She decided to be that someone, so she sat down and began thinking like a marketing person. She wrote ads, product descriptions, and promotional e-mails. The market responded, and sales increased. She was surprised to find out that she enjoyed the work. She would still say that she is basically a linear thinker; however, she has not restricted her work to that aspect. In fact, she now takes creative writing courses and writes short stories as a hobby.

This happens in the other direction as well. An artist finds he has a knack for finance. A visionary is able to work with others on the steps required for that vision. A marketer can plot step-by-step strategies. The point is, while you have a primary cognitive style, don't limit yourself.

The second problem you need to address with cognitive styles is the tendency to value one over the other. This happens in leadership circles, in business, and in literature. So the out-of-the-box thinker, who can think in terms of complexities and systems, is perceived as being more helpful to the organization than the linear thinker, who is seen as limited by A + B = C logic. On the other hand, the nonlinear thinker is criticized as irrational and unrealistic, even presumptuous, while the linear thinker is praised for attributes such as diligence and responsibility.

There is a danger to this sort of view, either way. It ignores the way leadership and organizations work. You need people with both cognitive styles. At different times in the company, the church, the family, or the small group, you may need one over the other, for that particular season. But both cognitive styles are necessary in the long term. New ideas need a sound basis in reality and vice versa.

So in terms of your own cognitive style, you most likely know which basic way your mind tends to work. The best direction is to continue honing your dominant cognitive style while appreciating and owning the other style as well.

This is important for your leadership because you need to harness and develop both cognitive styles as you lead the people around you. People need to follow someone who can help them with logical progression and also with nonlinear ability as their own situations and styles mesh with yours.

Thinking Relationally

Being a clear and productive thinker also requires the ability to craft thoughts and ideas in terms of relationships. Your mind didn't develop in a vacuum, apart from people. And it is a mistake to keep your thinking divorced from people—what they mean to you and how your thoughts will affect them. No matter what your area of leadership is, people are part of it. You lead people, you influence people, and you matter to people. Your organization has something to do with some service to people, whether a computer, a bank loan, a home, medical care, groceries, or a retail outlet. This means it's necessary to keep people in mind when you create opportunities and solve problems. This is true in two areas: connecting your thoughts and considering the impact of your thoughts. Let's take a look at these two aspects of thinking relationally.

Connecting Your Thoughts. Connecting your thoughts simply means bringing what you're thinking about to others. We are primarily designed to be relational beings, and real meaning and purpose derives from relationship. So the ideas, solutions, dilemmas, new visions, and improvements you come up with will do better when you talk about them with others. You engage with people, and they are drawn to what you are thinking. They are energized to your leadership. You, in turn, are enriched by their contributions.

This is why I love spending time with people who love what they do and think about what they do, especially if it's an industry I know nothing about. I enter a world, guided by an expert with many years of experience, that is not only interesting to me but is usually quite valuable in my own work. Not long ago, I had a long talk with a neighbor who sells rockets. I had no idea what was involved. He told me about the design issues, how spacecraft is marketed, the process of selling and negotiation, and how he leads his sales team in a very long track, taking years per sale. Later, as I thought about what he had told me, I was able to better look at the long-term perspective in my own work and company, which didn't compare with the perspective he has to have in his industry.

> The ideas, solutions, dilemmas, new visions, and improvements you come up with will do better when you talk about them with others.

This isn't to say that you shouldn't think at your desk, on a run in the hills, or while in a retreat setting. Thoughts that come in solitude can be very valuable. Whether you originate your ideas alone or in a meeting, make sure that on a regular basis someone, somewhere, knows what you are thinking. You aren't doing your spouse any favors when you get home and are asked how the day went, respond, "Fine." Get the ideas out; noodle them with her. If you do this regularly, you will think better and become more connected to her.

Considering the Impact of Your Thoughts. The other part of thinking relationally is considering the impact of your thoughts. Whatever group you are leading, it matters ultimately to people because people are what matter. You affect the end users of whatever you are producing. You matter to those end users. Keep those end users in mind at all times. They have difficult and complex lives. You want to provide something that makes those lives better in some way.

Even if you enjoy pure thought, you need to consider your impact on people because you matter to them. A friend of mine is extremely talented in mathematics. He could teach it on a university level. He is in business, however, and has led several successful companies by capitalizing on his math abilities, especially as applied to the financial world. A few years ago, he left a very good position for another one that, while it was also a success, wasn't at the intellectually stratospheric level of the first one. His reason for the job change was that he wanted a more direct route to the end user, more access to people, and more hands-on experiences. He sees both jobs as having equal value; it's not a case of better or worse. For him, it is a matter of wanting to see faces, eyes, and hands using a product he has created.

Even if you enjoy pure thought, you need to consider your impact on people because you matter to them.

This is what I mean by considering your impact. You will have an impact, one way or another. So keep your thoughts connected to relationships, and keep people's faces in front of you. There is no better way to have your thoughts integrated with the rest of your inner world than to be a relational thinker. I will deal more in depth with the relational world in chapter 4.

Reality with the Nod to the Positive

Another aspect of successful thinking is your orientation to reality. You think about what *is* going on, not what *you would like to be* going on. Reality happens, and it always wins. You must take the bad news with the good news even if it reflects poorly on you. This is the only way you will ever make transformational changes in yourself and in the people you work with.

In the church I attend, the leadership made a commitment several years ago to allocate a high percentage of funds to a children's ministry building. Their reasoning was that while there were other places to put money, the church is located in the middle of a growing community with lots of young families. They wanted to attract parents to come via the services the church had for the kids. These are leaders who are also committed to overseas work and fighting local poverty. They have high values to those needs, and it was hard to shift the finances during this time to a building. So it wasn't a reality they especially wanted to be true; it simply was what they believed to be true.

The leadership took a lot of criticism for this decision. People thought the money shouldn't go to brick and mortar but to direct services. The leaders listened to the complaints, but in time they went ahead with their decision. They were convinced of the reality that they could reach people in the best way by helping families get help. It was not a popular reality, but it was one they had researched and based their decisions on it.

You must take the bad news with the good news even if it reflects poorly on you.

Recently, a family with young children moved into our neighborhood. My wife and I invited them to church, and they went with us. While the grown-ups seemed to have a generally positive experience, it was the ten-year-old daughter who got their attention. When she returned from the children's ministry time, she told her parents she wanted to come back. Bear in mind here that she had moved to her new home from hundreds of miles away just two days before attending the church. She did not know a single soul there, but the warmth and quality of the program captured her heart. And many people in the community are now bringing their children for the same reasons.

The leaders thought in terms of reality, and they won in my book. They looked at what was, not what they wanted things to be. In your own leadership, face reality first. Get the bad news first. Really listen to the financial problems, personnel issues, and sales dilemmas. Good leaders think about reality first and then find solutions and opportunities second.

At the same time, I think the thoughts of a leader should ultimately go toward the positive. No one is completely balanced between good news and bad news. So veer toward hope. That is what a leader's thoughts bring to those who are watching and depending on him. They need someone who can bear the bad, contain it, understand the depth of it, and still provide a realistic hope if one exists. Certainly, if it's time to roll up the show, that is the reality. But a good leader brings thoughts to the table that look at every scenario that can provide something good for people.

All of us who desire to lead need to be mindful of the responsibility to have thoughts that are not only grounded in reality but also give hope at the end.

I have cohosted a daily call-in counseling radio show for many years, called *New Life Live!*[1] I have listened to thousands of callers present their struggles with troubled relationships, emotional issues, addictions, and the like. You face a lot of reality when you listen to people's personal problems. I often receive calls from individuals who have severe and complex problems, problems that certainly cannot be resolved in a few minutes on the phone. So I give them insights and perspectives for now, and then suggestions, steps, and resources for later, when the call is over. With the most hopeless-sounding situations, I have always tried to give something people could take away, something that was real and true and substantive, but also something that provided an option that they didn't have before they called. I don't know most of the endings of the stories. But I do know that all of us who desire to lead need to be mindful of the responsibility to have thoughts that are not only grounded in reality but also give hope at the end.

Holding Opposing Thoughts

Another mark of leaders who think well and successfully is that they are able to live in conceptual tension. They can listen to, and think about, ideas that are diametrically opposed. They have enough space in their minds that they can consider and analyze both sides while they are moving toward a decision.

This is not an easy task. We all have a tendency, as leaders, to think, *Plan A is better than plan B for these reasons, so let's go for A*. Because of the pressure and speed of leadership today, we simplify things to that level and move on. It becomes a zero-sum game: A wins and B loses. While that is often the right way to go, it is not always. The thinking leader must resist the impulse to immediately discard an idea that is antithetical to one he likes. He is apt to come up with better solutions, if he can live with the tension for a while.

I have a good friend who is a great example of this. He is a consultant for companies that are ready to go to the next level of growth. In a recent project with a group, he was interviewing vice presidents of different departments, as is his habit, to get an overall feel for the nature of the company. What he found was a large division between marketing and accounting. This is a typical tension: marketing wants enthusiastic support for their energy, and accounting wants to cut unwarranted expenditures. But this company was more divided than usual. The two departments had locked horns, and their adversarial relationship was actually the problem keeping the company from going to the next level. Marketing was convinced that the company was headed for a smaller market share, and ultimately disaster, if the company didn't make a big commitment to an aggressive ad campaign. Accounting saw no way that could work because the money was not there. The company was stretched thin as it was. There had been shouting matches and everyone calling on the CEO to take a stand on one side or the other. For his part, the CEO was torn, as he didn't know which answer was the right one. As the company's leader, he didn't want to alienate half the team by a decision, though he knew that might be the only answer.

> You have to at least think about two perspectives or opinions that don't agree. Don't immediately react and toss one out.

My friend the consultant coached the CEO in this way: "You may have to take sides on this. But I don't think you have to yet. Begin with the premise that both perspectives have a lot of merit, and see if there is some way you can go in both their directions." In other words, it might not be a zero-sum game. The CEO agreed to take some time to think about the issue. That was the beginning of the turning point for the company.

With this new idea of holding opposing thoughts at the same time, the CEO finally landed on a solution. It involved some infusion of capital, large enough that marketing could do some trimming and still mount a major campaign but small enough to satisfy accounting in case it backfired. The project worked, and the company did make it to the next level.

This doesn't mean you have to be open to absurdities. Some things just don't make sense. But it does mean that you have to at least think about two perspectives or opinions that don't agree. Don't immediately react and toss one out. Give your mind a little time to see if there is a win-win.

Adapting to New Realities and Truths

Related to this is the ability for the leader to change and adapt when the facts dictate it. The best leaders know that reality is larger than they are, so they don't mind taking a different course when there is new information. Clear thinking means submitting your mind to any new reality.

I was working in my office and needed to use a piece of computer equipment I'd left at home. I called one of my teenage sons and, knowing he was busy with school activities, offered him ten dollars to stop what he was doing and bring me the equipment. Since it was a thirty-minute round-trip drive, it sounded reasonable to me. He said, "I'll do it for fifteen dollars." I didn't mind that response. I didn't play the guilt card or the "you owe your Dad" card because I have talked to my sons a lot about money, time, and negotiation. I just said thanks but no thanks and hung up. Then I called his brother and left him a voice mail with the same request. I had a backup, having two sons who can drive.

About a minute later, the first son called me back and said, "I'll do it for ten dollars."

"Great," I said. "Why the change of heart?"

He said, "When I hung up, I asked Mom if you were trying to teach me a lesson on negotiation. She said, 'No, he's going to call your brother.'" My wife understood the situation clearly. And my son quickly adapted to the new information and made the necessary changes.

A leader who thinks well needs the ability to admit when he is wrong or should change direction. Those who insist that the original plan is the only plan are often at risk. You instill doubt in people with that stance, and you instill trust in people when you adapt to new realities.

Intuition: Your Mind Has a Gut

Let's return to a question I asked in the introduction of this book: *Have you ever ignored your gut and realized later that it was a mistake to do that?* I have asked many leaders this question over the years, and almost all of them admit they have had this experience. You most likely have as well. It is generally the same sort of story that goes something like this: You interview an individual to fill a position. The person looks great on paper; the résumé and recommendations are fine. He interviews well and seems to fit the bill. Yet you have some weird sense that something wasn't right about the person. You can't put your finger on it, but there is a negative response. However, with no rational reason to support that sense, you go ahead with the hire.

And then, within a few months, you find out what the weird negative response was about. It might be that the person has a poor work ethic; it might be a personality style that clashes with the wrong people; sometimes it is a character or moral problem. You can sense your gut tightening and chiding; your gut tightens and says to you, in so many words, *I told you so. Why didn't you listen to me?*

This sensation, often called *intuition*, is well known in leadership. It shows up in all aspects of life, however, such as buying a home, choosing whether or not to ask someone on a date, or discerning if your child is lying about where she's been. But its existence poses a problem:

How does the leader reconcile the two sorts of information: external and internal? What do you do with a sense or a response that doesn't seem to have a basis in facts? In a way, these questions represent the main idea of the book: How can you best use the internal sources of your life to lead well and successfully? I believe there is an answer to the question and that intuition can be a very helpful aspect of your leadership. So let's first understand what the word *intuition* means.

The experience of intuition is drawing a conclusion about a person or a situation with no known basis for that conclusion.[2] It is generally immediate and quick. Intuition tends to be direct: *Stop. Go. Yes. No. Do it. Don't do it.*

There are many theories about what intuition is: an emotional reaction, a conviction of some reality with an as-yet-undiscovered source for it, a mystic experience, the voice of God. However, a good deal of research now indicates that rather than being a mystical and unknowable process, intuition may be a combination of two elements of how we think and how we assimilate information. The first has to do with the analytical and logical parts of the mind, generally identified as the left brain. This is the part that is linear and quantitative in nature. This part seems to have the capacity to think extremely rapidly and come up with conclusions almost instantly. It's as if, in computer language, the processor speed is almost incalculable. This aspect of intuition is logical yet very rapid. For example, a radiologist can look at an x-ray and almost immediately conclude what is wrong with a person's spine. She has looked at thousands and thousands of x-rays. Her mind rapidly does the work because this is known territory. But if this same radiologist is looking at a stock report, without a lot of experience, she may deliberate for hours on what decision to make. This is how the more left-brain process works.

The experience of intuition is drawing a
conclusion about a person or a situation with
no known basis for that conclusion.

At the same time, intuition seems to also work from the right brain—the creative, more spontaneous part. This is that hunch that you can find no logical, informational, or data-based reason for. You just *know*, and you know that you know that you know. It is the classic hunch with no supporting evidence. This aspect of intuition seems to be simply another way of reaching conclusions that does not follow a linear path. The path is more emotional and experiential.

A married couple I know is a good example of right-brain intuition. As with many couples, he is more rational while she tends to be more intuitive. They work together in leadership in the same organization. He tells me that he will not interview anyone for a position or a proposal unless she is also in on the process. There have been so many instances in which she would say, "He's going to be a problem," or "Don't let her get away," and she would have a very high hit rate. She would not be able to articulate the reasons, but she had strong senses of yes or no. The husband, seeing the same interviewee, may see nothing of what she experienced. But he has learned to trust her "knowing without knowing."

Intuition does seem to work in areas in which you are competent and experienced. That is, when you know your subject well, your mind has many experiences, memories, patterns, and conclusions from which to draw. This experience base feeds the accuracy of the hunch.

Can Intuition Be Wrong?

From whatever side of the brain it originates, intuition is a kind of thinking process, and any thought can be mistaken. You can have the wrong facts, or you can draw the wrong conclusions on the right facts.

When I am consulting with leaders who believe it's best to always go with the gut every single time, I take them on a review of their past decisions. Sooner or later, we will find some instance in which intuition led them in a way that wasn't the best way. This includes even those, like the wife above, who have a very good track record.

Go Back to Reality

The best way any leader can use her mind to think in ways that work for her organization is to remember that *reality is in charge.* It is not divided. There are no inner and outer realities that are ultimately opposed. Both sources of truth must be subject to what is truly true. So in an ideal setting, your intuition should agree with your conscious thinking.

<hr>

Become a wise, sober-minded person of good judgment. Pay attention to what you see.

<hr>

When the two disagree, I believe there is generally something missing. For example, take the earlier instance of hiring a person you felt weird about. Most likely, you didn't have enough information about that individual at the time. If you had dug deeper into the recommendations, or observed him over a period of time in stressful situations, it's likely that the flaw would have emerged. Then your intuition and the objective information would have worked together. That is why many businesses hire with a probationary period, so that time will tell the tale without a lot of damage in case things don't work out. There is a Bible verse that says, "Do not lay hands upon [put into church leadership] anyone too hastily."[3] Significantly, this applies to the process of picking business leaders also. On the flip side, perhaps you felt great about a person who later proved to be a problem. In this case, there could be several reasons your intuition failed. You wanted his skill set so much you didn't pay attention to the warning signs. Or you tend to be overoptimistic and miss character flaws in others. Or perhaps you liked him as a person but didn't check out his skill set deeply enough.

The real takeaway here is to think, observe, and learn from the experience. If intuition is a type of thinking, then what helps conventional thinking to improve also helps intuition. The more experience you have, the more able you are to observe patterns in people, and the more you are able to learn from your observations, the better fuel you have to grow your intuitive abilities. That is how intuition grows and develops for you. Become a wise, sober-minded person of good judgment. Pay attention to what you see. Don't put intuition on a pedestal, but don't ignore it either. A well-trained intuition is a good servant and a poor master.

Creativity and Leadership

What would you give to have been a fly on the wall at different great moments in leadership, especially those in which a creative idea changed the whole paradigm? For example:

- Henry Ford comes up with a mass-produced car.

- Fred Smith starts Federal Express, a faster and more reliable way to ship goods.

- Bill Gates begins Microsoft at age nineteen.

- Pierre Omidyar lands upon a new business concept that becomes eBay.

Through the ages, leaders have always been associated with creativity. Creative leaders are valued, and their contributions make a difference. Your thoughts contain the potential to come up with creative ideas that can change and improve your organization, department, church, group, or family. Think about the last time someone in your organization came up to you and said, "We have a problem with X. What can we do?" Like most leaders, you probably felt the pressure that it is now your problem. You're the leader. You must come up with a solution that no one else has been able to. It's in your lap. That is real pressure. But your creativity can go a long way to coming up with a solution, a new take on things, or a new idea that can move your group forward.

What Is Creativity?

Creativity is, simply put, the ability to rearrange existing components into a new whole. That is, you take what you see, organize it in a different way, and come up with a new idea, a new solution, a new service, or a new product. Ford, Smith, Gates, and Omidyar all saw a need and an opportunity in business. Business was the context they were observing and thinking about. Sometimes it seems that creativity comes up with something out of nothing. Think, for example, of an artist in a windowless room who paints a masterpiece out of his head. However, that artist has memories and experiences to draw from. And that is what makes creativity so accessible: we all have the raw components lying around in our lives.

It used to be that creativity was viewed as an ability for only those who had a special gift. Either you were creative, or you weren't. While there certainly seems to be those individuals who are innately highly creative, it is now understood that everyone can create at some level. And in today's market and opportunities, that is an ability that every leader needs to develop. Here are some of the aspects of creativity that are relevant for leadership.

Creativity Can Operate Well Collaboratively

Creativity thrives when you are in relationship. Great ideas come out of people supportively tossing ideas around in a team. For example, the extremely popular PlayStation video games have more than one hundred people creating them in a team.[4] Solitude certainly plays a large part in the creative process since you need time away from distractions to think productively. But the more relational you are, the better input you can use from others, and the better feedback you receive for your own thinking.

Creativity Uses Your Leadership Context

As with the business examples above, creativity generally doesn't come out of a vacuum. It arises from opportunity and need. There is an environment, a context, a setting for the creative process. A creative leader learns to look at her situation and asks how this can be done better.

In the late 1980s, Dr. Henry Cloud invited me to partner with himself and psychiatrists Frank Minirth and Paul Meier in a medical and psychological treatment program company that would provide both inpatient and outpatient treatment on the West Coast of the United States. David Stoop, another psychologist, was also a partner with us. Part of the program was a teaching element, in which we taught a number of lessons to the patients at one of the hospital units. We instructed them about principles and insights on aspects of emotional and relational growth and healing, and we taught these lessons as part of the inpatient program. Some of the topics concerned depression, anxiety, addictions, intimacy, trust, relationships, and the spiritual life.

We wanted to also make what we had been learning about with the inpatient program available to people who weren't in a hospital setting but who wanted life to be better or to grow or heal in some area of life. We thought the information and approach could help people, no matter what their life settings. So we started thinking of ways to get the information out. We knew that in Southern California, where we are located, public seminars were popular in all sorts of areas: finances, health and fitness, cooking, relationships, and personal growth. So we rented a ballroom in a hotel and began speaking every Monday night on some topic of growth. One of us would lecture for an hour on a subject and then answer questions from the audience for another half hour. We called it Monday Night Solutions.

The talks seemed to meet a need, and enough people attended that we decided to continue it after a trial period. Ultimately, we conducted these talks for eighteen years, live, almost every week of the year. Today, we have partnered with a media company that provides satellite programming by subscription to several thousand churches in North

America. We now record the Monday Night Solutions talks in a studio, and the DVDs are sent to various churches via satellite.[5]

People sometimes ask how we thought of a creative idea like a weekly live talk. My answer is that we simply *rearranged some existing components into a new whole*. Experts have been giving talks for a long time. The need was there, and the idea came. The creativity lesson for me in this area was to see what was out there and see if it could be improved on.

Creativity Is Pro-Structure

There is a myth that the creative process can only be unleashed when you get away from all order, discipline, and parameters. People who believe this say that creativity must be as free as possible to express itself. This sort of thinking is not true, and it discourages leaders from investing in the process. Leaders know the value of structure in organizations. They aren't about to abolish all that in the hope that creativity might happen.

The reality is that creativity flourishes with structure. Creative freedom can exist within parameters. A brainstorming meeting with a flip chart occurs for a specified amount of time. People ask thought-provoking questions to get the creative process going.

A great example of the creative process within parameters is music. Any musician has to submit to the structure that there are musical scales with a finite number of notes. Chords sound good only when they are the right chords. Random chords can ruin a song. I have seen brilliant ideas form in the minds of button-down executives and in T-shirted artists. Certainly there can be a micromanaging scenario, in which the structure intrudes on the process. But structure helps creativity.

Creativity flourishes with structure.

Creativity Is Pro-Health

Another myth that can dissuade the leader from investing in the creative process says that creativity comes from misery and unhappiness. The movie *Amadeus* vividly portrays Mozart's out-of-control life. Van Gogh's brilliance is often associated with his madness. But the "tortured artist" idea doesn't hold up in reality. Creativity is enhanced by personal and emotional health and the growth process in general. It flourishes in a fulfilled environment.

Think of your mind as having a certain amount of room in it, like the RAM of a computer. RAM is used for the "thinking" a computer has to perform. The more RAM, the better the machine operates. When too many applications are open, however, there is less room, and the computer can become sluggish or inoperable. In a broad sense, the clearer your life and mind are, the more space creativity has to grow and bring new ideas.

A childhood friend of mine, Dr. Larry Bell, is an accomplished composer. A Juilliard graduate, he is chair of music theory at the New England Conservatory of Music and associate professor of composition at the Berklee College of Music. I visited Larry at a class reunion some time ago, and during our talk, I asked him about the "tortured artist" theory. He said, "It hasn't been true in my experience. When I went through very unhappy times in life, I didn't compose as well. And when my life and relationships have been fulfilling, I have done my best work." Larry's life and productivity are evidence that creativity is pro-health. As noted psychoanalyst Dr. Karen Horney has stated, "an artist can create not because of his neurosis, but in spite of it."[6] I like to ask people who hold to the tortured artist idea, "What if Mozart and van Gogh had had good lives? What works might they have produced then?" And the same is true for you. Health and growth are good for you and for your creative development.

Creativity Requires Intentionality

Creativity, especially for the leader, takes work and discipline. You must allot time, room, and energy for creativity, in both developing it and in using it. I recommend to leaders that they read up on creativity, learn from experts, and get to know the process. There are many structured experiences and exercises designed by creativity experts to help you look at matters from a different angle and build your creativity muscles.

Creativity, especially for the leader, takes work and discipline.

In your context, use creativity intentionally. In your work relationships, tell people you need to think about things creatively. Have meetings dedicated to finding a new way of taking advantage of an opportunity or solving a knotty problem. Don't make the mistake of waiting for the inspiration to come. It can and it does, certainly. All of us have had an *aha* experience of some kind. But that generally comes after you have made efforts beforehand that began the internal process already.

Pay Attention to Your Thinking

Become an observer of how you think. As I said, it may sound strange to think about thinking, but it is important and helpful. There are several patterns to be aware of.

Recognize Cognitive Distortions

Psychologists talk about *cognitive distortions*, or patterns of thinking that aren't reality-based and therefore hinder your productivity. I have written about them in more detail elsewhere.[7] There are several distortions that can hamper a leader's thinking. Look at the list below and see if you experience any of these patterns:

- *Helplessness*—the sense of "I've tried and nothing helps," as if there are no choices available to you.

- *Passivity*—a pattern in which you are afraid or hesitant to take initiative, so you wait for someone or some circumstance to provide the solution.

- *Negativity*—a well-known pattern in leaders in which there is an imbalance of negative over positive. It is often justified as being "realistic," but it is generally built on fear and failure, not reality.

- *Defensive thinking*—a scenario in which you are unable to own your own contribution to a problem or to see another person's feedback as superior, so you rationalize your position to the point of uselessness.

- *All-or-nothing thinking*—the idea that there is only one answer to a situation. This kind of thinking is very limited and is usually produced by anxiety or a perfectionist streak. Sometimes there is only one answer, but most of the time there are several. The best thinking occurs when you look at various scenarios and play them out, either in your mind or with others.

- *False self-thinking*—this occurs when you try to be someone you're not either to please people with that image or to keep yourself from seeing your own faults. It becomes a very restricted way of living and leading.

Observe Your Thoughts

Life is chaotic, and sometimes too much information can cause confusion in an organization. As a result, leaders are under great pressure to think with focus and direction. It is an important task.

Marcus Buckingham's writing on clarity has been a major contribution to helping people recognize how important it is for leaders to think clearly and to give clarity to those they lead.[8] Sometimes, however, leaders interpret a need for clarity as a need to control their thoughts and keep them directed and precise. This is a problem. The leader needs to provide clarity to the organization, but she needs to also observe where her thoughts are leading and what they mean. There is much value that can come from observing your thoughts.

For example, think about someone in your organization who, when you are engaged in a conversation with him for more than a minute or two, your thoughts begin to wander. It can be like the movie scenes where a bored high-school student enters some daydream while his teacher drones on, then startles back to reality when she stands over him, saying, "Do you understand my question?" When talking to this person at work, you find yourself thinking about golf, lunch, or your date that night. As a result, you miss what the other person is saying and have to quickly catch up somehow so he won't notice.

You may be tired. You may not be interested in the topic. But there are other reasons you may be thinking those particular imaginative thoughts. And if you understand those reasons, they can point to something valuable for you, the leader. For example:

- He rambles on about details no one cares about, and he needs to be coached to be succinct.

- He talks in an egocentric way about his own perceptions only, and he needs to be helped to consider other people's experiences and viewpoints.

- You are annoyed with him about something, so you detach from him via your imagination. You may need to rectify that.

- He is bringing you negative news you don't want to hear. You may need to hear it anyway.

- You can't sufficiently detach from whatever you were doing and pay attention to him. You may need to refocus on him and return to the previous issue after the conversation.

The point is, look at not only *what* you are thinking but *how* you are thinking. This process will pay off for you in the long term.

Thinking Leader Thoughts

Leaders must think differently. They must think as a leader, with "leader thoughts." What I mean by that is that a leader's job is not only to connect with people and inspire them to greatness, but also to think in ways that prove that he or she has earned the hat of leadership. This is the world of ideas. You have the hat because you are expected to have ideas that others don't have.

During the presidential campaign at the time of this writing, we see a great deal of emphasis on which candidate has the best ideas. Certainly the candidates' personality, warmth, and maturity play a large part. But people want to see who has the best ideas concerning the economy, national defense, taxes, health care, and a host of other areas. When a candidate mentions a new solution, it makes the national news.

This doesn't mean that you, in your context, need to have all the best ideas. But you do need to create a setting where the best ideas come. Sometimes that may mean bringing in someone who has the best ideas. Recruiting an expert is a good idea in itself. It is also what good leaders do.

This doesn't mean that you, in your context, need to have all the best ideas. But you do need to create a setting where the best ideas come.

You need to be ahead of the pack. You need to think further ahead than those you lead, so you can look beyond what is going on now. Your thoughts, your leader thoughts, can move your organization to a new place of success because you took the time to think like a leader.

One aspect of thinking the thoughts of a leader is that you need the ability to be *free*. By that, I mean the ability to choose when and how you will decide on a matter. A leader who is free listens to others, analyzes situations, and tolerates pressure from others to act immediately, to decide right now. If you are the leader, you have the prerogative to freely consider the matter, to think about and discuss the alternatives and choices, and then to decide on your course and your timetable. If your thoughts are bound up in taking responsibility for the anxiety of others, you aren't free, and you can't operate as a leader. Thinking leader thoughts requires asserting, in a kind way, that you will choose what you will choose, when you choose it.

Having presented the importance of understanding thinking, we now move to an exciting but controversial area in leadership in the next chapter: the place of emotions. A central part of the inner life, your feelings can be a great asset to you in what you do.

Chapter Three

EMOTIONS

The Unlikely Allies in Leadership

I was talking to Alan, an executive who was in charge of several departments. He was telling me that he had an "attitude problem" with one of his direct reports, a manager.

"What kind of attitude problem?" I asked.

"Well, I get frustrated easily with him," he said. "Sometimes I even get angry with him, though I don't like to admit it. I don't think I'm being fair about this. I'm not that way with anyone else who reports to me, just him. I wish I could get over this attitude. I just need to stop being mad."

"That may be," I said. "But let's look first at what's going on. What do you get frustrated about with him?"

Alan said, "Well, actually, lots of things. He's a nice guy, and people like him. And he is valuable to the company. But he is so disorganized. I can't get information from him when I need it. He doesn't get his reports in on time. He's like a traffic jam in the company; everything slows down because of him."

I said, "Then there may be good reason for your frustration. What have you done about it?"

"I've talked to him a million times, but his behavior doesn't change.

So I have to spend more time managing this manager than I do everyone else combined." Then Alan returned to his original thought. "But I don't like being angry like this. Show me some way to turn the anger around."

"Let me suggest something else," I said. "Maybe you *should* be frustrated and angry."

"Should be? But I'm not an angry type of guy."

I said, "That's my point. You're no raving rageaholic. You're a pretty even-keeled person, I know that. So maybe what's going on should be bothering you, and it's telling you to fix the problem."

"Fix it how?"

"Well," I said, "somehow you need to arrange things differently. There are several ways you might do this. You can find a way in which he gets his act together. Or you find someone who can manage him so you don't have to. Or you can find him another area to work in that doesn't require that he be organized. Or he may have to leave. But one way or another, I don't think the solution is to stop being angry. It's to *fix what is making you angry.*"

Your emotions can be your friend and your ally as a leader.

Alan thought about it and got it. He went to work on the situation. And in time, what worked was the second suggestion. Alan had the person report to someone else, who then reported to Alan. As a result, Alan's "attitude problem" went away. He wasn't frustrated and angry anymore. The new supervisor certainly had a challenge, but he had more time to allocate to the person than Alan did, so he wasn't as bothered. The individual did pretty well in the new situation and even became somewhat more structured because of the new arrangement.

Here is the point: your emotions can be your friend and your ally as a leader. When you lead beyond reason, you also seek out your emotions and utilize what they bring you. This chapter will present ways to do just that.

The Stepchild of Leadership

As a leader, how do you view your feelings? Do you enjoy them? Look forward to them? Discuss them frequently? Probably not. If you are like most people in leadership, you most likely look at your emotions with some reserve. Leaders, to a large extent, have learned from experience that emotions are something that are to be controlled and mastered, and not much more than that. Emotions are rarely seen as accelerating leadership abilities. They are the stepchild of leadership.

In leadership circles, you hear "I'm interested in what you think about . . ." more than "I'm interested in how you feel about . . ." More value is attributed to the cognitive part of the inner world than to the emotional part. It is part of the leadership culture. That is why I was struck by Jeff's comment about fear that I mentioned in the introduction to this book. Sometimes leaders describe a thought as a feeling (a typically male phenomenon). For example, he will say, "I feel that we need to allocate more resources to marketing." But that is not an accurate representation of what emotions are. Emotions aren't ideas; they are internal responses.

There are, of course, good reasons for this hesitation. We all have seen situations in which a leader gave vent to some emotion and made a huge error in judgment. Or in other situations in which fear and anxiety caused a leader not to move forward boldly, and bad outcomes followed. Or when at other times, intense feelings alienated a leader from those close to him. The leader who has constant emotional displays tends to create a negative impression of his competence.

I was recently called up to be on jury duty. I took a few days off work and listened to the arguments of the plaintiffs and the defense. At the end of the arguments, the judge ordered us to deliberate and come up with a verdict. As part of her instructions to us, she said, "You may have had emotional reactions to the people you have listened to. But don't let your emotions cloud your judgment." And she was right in saying that. Some of the jury members had a negative response to the style of one of the people in the trial. We had to keep refocusing ourselves on what the law said, what the truth was, and what the real issues were. It was the only way we could deliver a verdict that we thought was just and fair.

Having agreed, then, that emotions can present a real problem in leadership, I want to present the other side and show that emotions not only can be helpful but also are a necessary part of successful leadership. Remember that in the introduction, I said *you ignore what is beyond reason to your peril*. That warning is probably most true in this arena of the emotional world.

What are *emotions* or *feelings*? (In this book, I am using the two terms as synonyms, not in a technical sense.) A good working definition is that emotions are *subjective reactions*. Emotions include positive reactions, such as tenderness, happiness, or satisfaction. They also include negative reactions, such as anger, anxiety, or sadness. Emotions can be intense, or they can be subtle. They can be absolutely overwhelming, or we can be totally unaware that we are having them.

Emotions not only can be helpful but also are a necessary part of successful leadership.

Like anything else inside you, emotions don't exist of and for themselves. Your emotions have a function, a purpose, a role. When you understand this role, you can use your emotions well to lead others to success.

The Signal Function

Your feelings exist as a signal to you. They alert you that something is going on, something you need to pay attention to and deal with. That *something* may be an event outside of you or one inside. Look at your emotions as you would the instrument panel on your car. On the panel are gauges and indicators that read out information on fuel, engine temperature, RPM, oil, and tire pressure. When the indicators are in the proper range or are simply not turned on, you don't think a lot about them because they signify that things are going normally. But when the indicators go into the red, blink, beep, or light up, you pay attention because they are alerting you of a situation that needs to be taken care of.

In one of my first full-time jobs, I drove a company car about thirty miles with the oil light on. In my ignorance, I assumed it was like the gas gauge, and I figured I had awhile before the oil was out. But by the time I barely made it back to the job site, the car needed major repairs. My boss was undeservedly kind to me about my foolishness, but he did sit me down and explain what to do the next time the oil light went on.

That is what emotions do for you, and why it's good to understand what they mean and what to do about them. They point to a situation. Most of the time, there is some action you can take that will resolve the situation. The result is that the emotion gradually resolves in its intensity. Its job is done, so the emotion dissipates until the next time.

Take Alan's frustration and anger in the opening illustration of this chapter. Alan wanted to stop having the emotions of anger. He didn't like feeling them. That is understandable. These are unpleasant emotions. No one wants to be angry all the time. His own solution, of trying to not be angry, would be like taking a hammer to the oil light, smashing it, and then saying, "OK, that problem is solved." But the real problem, the situation that caused the light, isn't solved and will get worse over time. So instead, when Alan distanced himself from the disorganized individual, the frustration and anger went away, not because Alan chose to not feel them but because he solved the real problem.

There are schools of thought that say that you can simply choose to feel, or not to feel, certain emotions. The theory is that feelings always follow our thoughts. So if you change your perspective, then your feelings will follow suit. Could Alan have learned more patience with his direct report and been less angry? He could have, in time. If he had had no other options available to him, he may have had to do that. Sometimes that does help us, as we grow, to become more mature and have a larger view on things. But that isn't always the best thing to do with our feelings. The best thing is to first look at the meaning of the emotion, see what causes it, and then deal with that.

Emotions aren't always a signal of something "out there" going on. They can also alert you to something happening within you. You have a tough day, and when you get home, you snap at your kids for being kids. You encounter several difficult sales calls and feel discouraged when the next client offers a little resistance. You hear that your new boss is difficult, so you become anxious when she asks for a meeting, only to find that she wants your advice. Though it is natural to think your feelings are telling you about someone or something, this is not what mature leaders assume. It is what children think. Not only that, but you are also to determine if the feeling actually has something to do with you. This is always the best first step.

> Emotions aren't always a signal of something "out there" going on. They can also alert you to something happening within you.

Negative Emotions

It is helpful for leaders to understand what specific emotions mean because they have individual messages and information for you. Then you can more easily trace what you are feeling to what is going on, to determine your course of action. Let's take a look at a few of the negative feelings we have and what they convey to us.

Anxiety

Anxiety is a sense of unease, fear, or dread that signals you to move away from something or someone. It is a sign of danger or a lack of safety. Sometimes it comes out in physical ways, such as a queasy stomach, sweaty palms, or a rapid heartbeat. Anxiety is a helpful emotion because it warns you that you may be in a situation that is not good for you. Many leaders have experiences in which they ignored their anxiety and made an error as a result.

A friend of mine told me that he found himself dreading any interaction with his boss. He avoided the man and tried to cut any conversation short. I asked him why, and he said, "He's really distant with me; he's not friendly. I don't think he likes me."

I knew his boss, and I didn't think he was that kind of a person. I also knew that he did like my friend; in fact, he had told me so. I said, "Is it possible that he's a little reserved? Maybe his seeming distance is not directed at you. I have always seen him as simply a little on the quiet side."

Many leaders have experiences in which they ignored their anxiety and made an error as a result.

My friend's previous supervisor had been a very gregarious and warm person, the kind of person who really got to know others and meant it. Thinking about it, my friend said, "It could be; I never thought about it."

I suggested, "Why don't you make the first move and ask him how things are? Maybe he needs that."

That pretty much solved the problem. My friend started taking the initiative with his boss, against his own personal reaction. He would simply walk up to his boss and ask how the weekend had been or what his plans were for that night. The result was that the boss began warming up to him, and their relationship markedly improved. Certainly it would have been better had the boss done the initiating himself, but that wasn't the situation. So in this case, the anxiety signaled that my friend was interpreting his boss's reserve as dislike. And when he took the action step, he solved the problem, which then resolved the anxiety.

There are other times, however, when the anxiety signals a real-time, actual, and objective danger to be avoided. In these instances, instead of powering through, we need to stop, feel the feeling, understand the source, and take the right action steps.

For example, some time ago, I was approached by a man with a business offer. He wanted me to invest with a communications company that was starting up with a new concept. It seemed to be quite sound and a very good idea, with lots of upside. The only hitch was that he needed for me to make a decision very quickly. As he said, "The ship is leaving the dock."

I needed more time to do due diligence and research the situation. At the same time, I hated missing what could be a great opportunity. So I tried to get as much information as I could in the little time I had. As I thought about the matter, I realized I was becoming anxious. I was feeling some fear about what was going on. At first, I thought I was just having the normal jitters before taking a risk. But it didn't go away. It got worse. In fact, the anxiety quickly became greater, in my mind, than my initial excitement about the opportunity. Finally, I figured out the nature of the anxiety: *I did not have sufficient time to get enough information to commit.* I wanted to say yes, but I could not. So I had to say no.

It turned out that my anxiety did me a favor, as the company didn't fare well. Anxiety says avoid this or go the other way, and I did. But again, the anxious feelings weren't the issue. They simply pointed to the reality I had to face, which was that I was being asked to rush to judgment. For many of us, the fact that someone doesn't give you a lot of time to decide is a warning sign that there is trouble. Maybe it should have been for me. Regardless, the illustration points out how helpful your anxiety can be, if you listen to it.

Anger

We experience anger as a call to address conflict. When we sense an obstacle to be faced or a wrong to be righted, our energy level rises, and we prepare to confront or combat the situation in some way. The best way to understand anger is that it signals to us there is a problem to be solved. It urges us to fix something that needs to be fixed. Again, anger can be from the outside or inside, but it must be addressed and dealt with. What makes us angry is not always a bad person, but at least a bad situation we want to see changed. We don't like to see people we care about getting hurt. Or diligently planned projects go south. Or our efforts to reach out to someone result in us being blamed or attacked. These situations often provoke an angry response. This emotion can last a few seconds, or it can run for days and weeks. But the idea is that your anger is urging you to deal with a problem.

As I mentioned at the beginning of the chapter, there are many war stories about a raging executive yelling, intimidating people, and slamming his fist on the desk. He is certainly engaged in battle, but most of the time, his anger is not solving anything. People sometimes talk about how good it is to vent anger. While it's good to bring anger into relationship, in order to connect it and understand it, the act of venting, in and of itself, is overrated. A person with a chronic anger problem can vent all day and then get up the next morning and do it again. He has something going on inside that he needs to deal with, and it's going to require "more than counting to ten," as a colleague of mine, Kay Yerkovich, once said.

To look at how anger works, let's return to the example of Alan and his direct report. As it happened, Alan's anger was a normal reaction to an external situation. But it could have been different. Suppose, for example, the manager was working fine and wasn't causing any problems. But Alan was constantly finding himself annoyed when he talked to him. That might point to something inside Alan, an alert of a different nature. It might have been that the man had some trait or style that was a hot button for Alan. Say he was somewhat chatty, and Alan liked people to get to the point. There would be nothing wrong with the person, but Alan just didn't like that style. In that case, the action step would probably be a different one, something like understanding where that annoyance came from. Maybe Alan had a previous boss who never got down to brass tacks and Alan couldn't get clarity from him, and that experience stayed with him. Then, having understood the source, Alan could forgive that previous boss, let it go, and find more tolerance for his direct report.

It could go the other way also. Suppose the manager was a very direct and to-the-point person while Alan preferred a little conversation before getting to matters. The direct report would seem cold and abrupt to him. Then Alan would have to figure out why he reacted that way to that style. The point here is simply that it may be about the situation. And it may be about you. As a leader, you need to be open to either direction. Just remember the problem-solving nature of anger. Don't avoid it. Don't let it control you. Be sure to find its source, and take action.

Sometimes you find yourself feeling angry about a leadership problem, and there is nothing you can do to fix it. Your anger may have helped you to work hard to resolve things, but some matters, no matter how we try, don't always go how we want. We can't solve every problem and we can't win 100 percent of the time. I think we can win a great deal of the time, but anyone who says we can bat a thousand doesn't live in the real world.

In these cases, your anger may have done its job and run its course. When you have done everything you knew to do, been as creative as possible, received lots of sound advice, gone the third mile, persisted, and prayed, then it may be time to move past anger and problem-solving. Otherwise the anger keeps you frustrated and beating your head against the wall.

Some matters, no matter how we try, don't always go how we want.

This is the situation of the leader who continues being annoyed about something he needs to let go of. He brings up an unchangeable problem over and over again, it takes over his thoughts like an obsession, and his colleagues get tired of hearing about it. He is stuck in what psychologists call a *protest stance*. He is still arguing his side in his mind and unable to get past it. You will often hear this person say things such as, "It can't be; it shouldn't be; maybe if I try it this way" about a situation that won't change. He is protesting a situation he needs to let go of. His anger is driving him to continue fighting, but it is not a wise use of his anger. Instead, it may be time for him to change, adapt, and go another direction. And that sort of protest anger has its final resolution in the next emotion I want to present: sadness. It is not the most popular emotion for leaders, but it is a vital one to experience and understand.

Sadness

Sadness is a feeling of grief and mourning. We feel despondent or regretful. We shed tears and sometimes isolate ourselves. Sadness has its own signal and message, which is that we are experiencing loss. Something or someone we value and care about has left us. It's all about the process of grieving.

There are many victories and many losses you will experience in life and in leadership. That's just the way life is, and it's normal. A deal you dreamed of doesn't come through, no matter how hard you tried to make it work. A person who is driving you crazy will not listen to reason and persists in how he behaves. Market forces turn everything upside down, and things beyond your control affect your work. A window of opportunity you didn't take advantage of in time is now closed to you. You make a judgment call, and it's the wrong one.

On a more personal level, there are also many losses people experience. A marriage ends. A loved one passes away. Your children go down the wrong path and cause you heartache. You make mistakes in how you treat people you love, and you alienate them. You encounter health problems. You develop a bad habit that you regret. You wonder where God is, in all of this, and if He cares.

As a leader, you may be tempted to skip over this section. It deals with something negative, the feeling of sadness, which seems counterintuitive to the leadership experience and direction. As I said, sadness is not the most popular emotion for the leader. Leaders focus on value and outcomes. What value and what outcomes can arise from being sad? Doesn't that lead to slowing down, stagnation, a pity party, blaming, and even depression? Better to keep moving, cut your losses, and keep positive.

In my work with leaders over time, I have come to understand this perspective. Leaders are under tremendous pressure to be an example, an inspiration, a positive force, and a source of energy to their organization. That is the reality, and it is the right thing. It is an essential of leadership.

At the same time, there is another essential, and that is to be able to handle losses, as well as the corresponding emotion of sadness, for they will happen. Loss is part of life, the way the world is. Losses have three sources: you, others, and the world. Your own failures and lapses in judgment can cause a loss. Others in your life can be the source. And sometimes, the economy, the weather, or an illness that is no one's fault can cause it. More often than not, the losses you experience are some combination of the three. But remember that as a leader, you will lose. It is a fact. How you deal with loss separates the winners from the losers. Ironically, those who can't deal with loss ultimately lose. And those who know how to deal with loss will win. Here is how that works.

Sadness is the emotional signal of the reality of loss. It says, *I lost. Maybe someone else won, maybe not, but I know I lost. And I lost something I wanted.* Whether you lost a position, a venture, a financial gain, or a relationship, sadness connects you with whatever you wanted. It is about desiring something, most likely something good. And desire, wanting something, feeling a longing for something, is necessary for sadness and grief. If you don't desire or care about anything, you will never have to feel sadness. There is nothing to lose, so there is nothing to let go of.

People who are detached from their desires, their cares, their hearts, and their relationships often are spared of feeling sad. But that is not a good way to live. In fact, very detached people often suffer from relational problems, intimacy issues, and clinical depression. Not wanting or caring about something, for the purpose of avoiding sadness, is to miss the point of leadership in the first place. Leadership is about wanting to make a difference, having a vision, helping people you care about, changing lives, and meeting goals. Desire and care keep you moving on that path. You can't have one without the other. Desire and sadness must coexist in your inner life.

How you deal with loss separates the winners from the losers.

So what good is sadness then? Here is its value: *sadness tells you to let go and move on.* It points you to the reality that you can't have something you desire, at least today, and you need to go another route. Give up trying to put a square peg in a round hole. Stop trying to make the deal work that can't work. Realize that person is the wrong one for the job, though you desperately need someone in that position. If you have someone in your small group who wants to leave, and you've had several conversations to try to work it out, let the person leave and wish him favor. Set a goal this next year that is more realistic than the one last year that was impossible.

I think there is tremendous value in paying attention to your sad feelings. Then you're not stuck like the man I mentioned before, lost in the mode of "It can't be; it shouldn't be; maybe if I try it this way . . ." That begins to sound like a love-smitten person who, when rejected, starts stalking his ex. You don't want that kind of existence. It isn't the path to success.

The main reason I think leaders have a particularly tough time with this emotion is that *sadness means you are helpless to change some reality.* I don't mean that you are completely and totally helpless. Certainly you have options and choices, but there are times you must accept that you are helpless to change someone or something. Here are some examples of what you may say "I can't change this" about. You might be helpless in:

- making someone change their negative opinion of you;
- resurrecting a deal that has gone away;
- causing someone to stay who wants to leave;
- keeping a position that is no longer an option;
- going back into the past and doing things again differently.

Leaders resist helpless situations; it's not what they signed up for in leadership. That is understandable. Leaders are workers and doers. But as I said, this isn't complete and total helplessness. It has limits and parameters. You can always go another way to achieve what you want to achieve. It is helpful to become accustomed to the reality that we are not God. Your sadness points you to a consigned and limited helplessness that will help you face your loss and move to those matters in which you can be helpful and effective.

During the past several years, Dr. Henry Cloud and I have conducted a weeklong training experience for leaders called the Ultimate Leadership Workshop.[1] In these workshops, Henry and I teach the attendees principles on leadership, values, the internal world, and reaching outcomes. Another component of the week is that the leaders go into small group settings, where they unpack themselves, get real, and learn to take the information they are learning that eighteen inches from their heads to their hearts.

One of the biggest takeaways that the attendees tell us about in their feedback is that they have a new respect for the value of sadness. Now, these are motivated, highly competent, values-driven, and accomplished people. But they, inevitably, did not have the skills to handle loss. No one had ever helped them with that aspect of life, work, and leading. Here are a few examples of what they say:

- "I've been holding on to a demand to be perfect in all things. I'm learning to let that image go, as it will never happen. I'm learning that excellence doesn't demand perfection, and I have a new perspective."

- "I thought I could keep everyone in my company happy if I tried hard enough. I've let it go, and I'm becoming free of that trap."

- "I've had some business failures that I could not stop beating myself up about. I've allowed myself to feel the sadness, and instead I can now see them as learning experiences for my future."

- "I miss my team in my previous job, and I'm letting the sadness happen so that I can move on. Now I have more energy and encouragement to continue with the new group."

- "I've had some relational losses, and I never let myself say good-bye emotionally. I never got over that person, and it affected my work. I've now gone through the grief, and I'm back to my old self."

Sadness can help you move on to new opportunities and new challenges. Though it is a negative emotion, it has positive benefits. I talked to an executive who had transitioned from one company to another. When I asked him how it was going, he said, "I like the company I'm with, but I haven't really been excited about it or engaged there."

I said, "Any idea why?"

He told me, "I realized that I transitioned very quickly. I was with my former company for a long time, and I had a lot of relationships and experiences there. I don't think I ever gave myself time to let it go and grieve it."

From a time and resource perspective, sadness has a good return on investment. It is a temporary process. It finishes and resolves. It allows you to free up energy and motivation in your mind to lead the way you want to. And it helps you learn lessons from the past that are valuable.

Sadness can help you move on to new opportunities and new challenges. Though it is a negative emotion, it has positive benefits.

Sometimes I will talk to leaders who have no value for sadness. They will say, "Just get over it." I can understand that in some cases. For example, if someone is complaining endlessly about a situation that is long past and is yesterday's news, they do need to get over it. If their sadness concerns a problem that isn't a big issue, they do need to get over it. That is true about matters that don't really matter to you. You change an office in the same building. You train for a new specialty. These are changes that simply require adaptation and flexibility. They don't tend to generate a lot of sadness because there's not a significant loss involved. Or if some failure you experience isn't a big deal, you just dust yourself off and get back on the horse.

However, sometimes "just getting over it" will make things worse for you over time. If you have lost something or someone truly important to you, you will most likely have sad emotions about the loss. It's best to give it the value it deserves by allowing some time to be sad. It will do you good, and you will move on from there.

Finally, stay up-to-date on your grief and losses. Don't let them go unattended for a long time. Keep current with them. The sooner you grieve something, the less time it will take to let it go. It may be a couple of minutes. It may be much longer, if it's a significant loss. But the longer you put it off, the longer it will take to finally finish it. Jump into the grief process, and you will jump back into normal life that much sooner.

Guilt and Shame

The emotions of guilt and shame can slow down the energy, motivation, and creativity of a leader if they are not understood and dealt with. Though grief and shame are different in a technical sense, they are best described broadly as *an attack on yourself, by yourself.* You condemn or judge yourself harshly for violating a standard, for failing, for letting someone down, for not being sufficient, or for hurting someone, to name a few infractions. Further, this attack on yourself can be about something that is either true or simply perceived. You can beat yourself up, for example, as a loser when you hit a triple but expected to hit a homer.

Guilt and shame often are associated with self-judgment. Here are a few examples that leaders experience:

- *You don't know what you're doing in this job. You're a loser.*
- *If people knew how incompetent you were, you would be gone.*
- *Your last mistake really hurt a lot of people.*
- *You continually disappoint others and let people down.*
- *You give up too easily.*
- *You don't learn anything from what people are trying to tell you.*
- *The organization's struggles are all your fault.*

It doesn't take a lot of these self-statements to cause great discouragement and leadership paralysis. But it is a common reality that many leaders experience. So as we're dealing with our emotions, instead of trying to get rid of guilt and shame feelings, we need to understand their signal function so we can chart the way to resolving them.

Instead of trying to get rid of guilt and shame feelings, we need to understand their signal function so we can chart the way to resolving them.

There is nothing wrong with feeling bad when you fail. It means that you live in reality. When you succeed, you should celebrate. When you err, having negative feelings like disappointment, remorse, and concern for others shows you care about people, your responsibilities, and your leadership. Have you ever talked to someone who made huge mistakes that cost the organization a lot of money, and the person shrugged it off with, "Oh well, it will be better next time"? I have, and I don't trust these people with my time or my money. They aren't people who consider their accountability to others to be a grave matter. They are problem people. They are not examples of healthy, guilt-free living.

Guilt and shame are much worse than being disappointed or remorseful. They keep you reliving the past, in recriminations, and they paralyze you. When you experience these feelings, you need to look at what is going on. Most of the time, these emotions are signaling to you one of several issues, with their corresponding action steps:

- Your standards are unrealistic and need to be modified and adapted to what is normal.

- You are overidentifying with your error and think that it speaks to who you are as a person in general, rather than being simply a mistake that you, a normally competent person, have made.

- You have a deficit of accepting, safe, loving relationships with people who can help you feel loved and OK about yourself, and you need a few of these around you.

- You create parent figures out of the people around you and imagine that they are more disappointed in you than they actually are. You need to talk to them about how they really see you.

- You take too much responsibility for the job, the results, and everything in between so that when there is a failure, it's all your fault. You need to bear your own burden of leadership and be responsible for yourself while at the same time allowing others to take responsibility for themselves.

As you can see, these attitudes can slow down your progress and growth as a leader. But these action steps can take you a long way toward ending self-attacks and replacing them with loving self-correction that we can all use and benefit from.

As we've dealt with anxiety, anger, sadness, and guilt and shame, it's important to know that I am describing *normal* experiences of these emotions, along with *normal* action steps that resolve them. Sometimes, however, these emotions can become very intense and painful, and sometimes they do not resolve over time. If you are following these recommendations and are finding that the feelings are still disrupting your life with no relief over time, it may be that the issue they are signaling is deeper or more serious than you thought. That means you may have a clinical problem, in which there is an injury or emotional deficit that needs professional help and healing with a good psychologist. I know many leaders from all over the world who have received great personal benefit from psychotherapy and have found that their work and results improve as well.

Positive Emotions

Now I want to point out three of the primary positive emotions that leaders experience. Again, just as all emotions do, positive feelings function as a signal to you; they aren't an end in themselves. So it is just as important with positive emotions as it is with the negative ones to understand what they mean for you and your leadership.

Warmth
Warmth is a feeling that you have about relationships in your life. It draws you to move toward people you care about and engage with them.

Warmth can exist in any sort of relationship: romantic, friendship, or family. It simply is an emotion that makes you want to be close to or in the presence of another person. It can lead you to a satisfying conversation with your spouse, a great time playing with your kids, a stimulating night with your date, or a jog with a friend. Warmth reconnects you to people.

As a leader, you may be tempted to think, *If it's not broke, don't fix it. Why analyze warmth? Just enjoy it.* It is certainly an emotion to be appreciated and experienced, no doubt about it. But there is also value in understanding what warmth is telling you. Basically, warm feelings signal that this person is bringing you good. That is, he or she is providing some things for you that you need, some part of the fuel that you will need in some form for the rest of your life. The warmth helps you pay attention to that fuel so that you will not neglect it.

Think about the last good meal you ate in a restaurant. Most likely, that thought makes you want to make plans to return. The meal brought good fuel to you. Warm feelings remind you to get back to the connections you have.

Work is important, but relationship must be first.

As you most likely know, leaders are somewhat vulnerable to being workaholics or too task-oriented. Business demands and schedules can take up huge amounts of time. It is easy to run on fumes and become detached from the people you need and who also need you. Warm feelings remind you of the importance of relationships. They make you want to connect, to talk, to be intimate, and to care for someone who, in turn, cares for you. In my own work, when I am flying to speak at a conference, I will find myself thinking of my family and the people I care about. And the warm emotions that come out will balance what all the frantic activity points toward: people.

If warm feelings aren't something you experience on some sort of regular basis, consider that a problem. We certainly have to work, focus, concentrate, strategize, problem-solve, motivate, and inspire. These are the task-based parts of leadership. But if there aren't some moments during the day when you have warm feelings, look at a couple of possibilities. One is that you don't have enough of a support system in your life (we will deal with this in more depth in the next chapter), so you are somewhat detached and disconnected. Another is that you have difficulty letting people in or trusting them emotionally, so you cut off the warm feelings in order to stay safe from hurt. This may indicate a need for professional counseling, to help you learn to open up safely. Another is that you have a high value for tasks and a low one for relationships; you are more comfortable doing than relating. If this is the case, you may need to reorient your values so that relationship gets first place, and work gets second. Work is important, but relationship must be first.

Satisfaction

Satisfaction is an emotion that relates to work, accomplishment, and performance. It is a feeling of contentment that we have completed a task we are proud of. We can look back at the achievement and say to ourselves, *This was very much worth the effort.*

Leaders enjoy and relish those moments. They are a quiet celebration and reflection on the effort it took and the results that were produced. You may feel satisfied with a positive quarterly earnings statement, a building project that is now complete, a project your team did well, or a tough problem in your small group that you helped someone come through and have a better life.

When leaders don't experience satisfaction, they often become driven and frenetic.

What does satisfaction signal? I believe this emotion points out two things for you. The first is that you can stop now! Work and leadership need closure. There should be some points at which you know that a task is done, whether it took five minutes or five years. You can't keep up the pace, nonstop, without satisfaction telling you that you can rest and turn the page. When leaders don't experience satisfaction, they often become driven and frenetic. They are productive, to some extent, but it's ultimately a recipe for misery.

The other direction that satisfaction points us to is that work and leadership should bring a measure of fulfillment and joy. Your success should be a cause for satisfaction. The emotion then serves as a sign that life can be good and also that you can continue down the track to the next challenge. Without that emotion, work could become drudgery. Satisfaction is a signal that you are producing something and will continue to do so.

Happiness
While satisfaction is the feeling associated with results and accomplishment, happiness is the emotion that is concerned with anything

good that happens to you. It has nothing to do with whether or not you accomplished anything. That is, happiness is a sense of well-being and contentment in general.

Of all the emotions you have, happiness is the one that is most dependent on your circumstances and least dependent on you as a person. It is basically a response to positive things happening: a job you enjoy, a marriage that is fulfilling, a child who is doing well, a charity you are involved with, a hobby that is fun, good weather, a good meal, a funny movie. Happy feelings simply go with happy events. It doesn't take a lot of character or maturity to feel happy when happy things happen.

There are some dispositionally happy people. They simply have a positive emotional outlook. They are not bothered by things that bother other people. It's not that they are in denial or are pretending inside; they really feel that way. Most of the time, it is because they have experienced a long pattern of significant loving and secure relationships. Those experiences tend to provide a happier viewpoint. But that is not our focus here, as we are dealing more with the pure feeling of happiness itself.

Of all the emotions you have, happiness is the one that is most dependent on your circumstances and least dependent on you as a person.

How does understanding happiness apply to your life as a leader? What is your takeaway? The first is to look at what made you happy for those few minutes and *be grateful for that event*. Gratitude means that you appreciate what just happened to you. You don't dismiss or ignore it. You don't say, "Well, what's next?" and move on. You experience thankfulness for it. You tell people who were involved in the event how much you appreciate them. There really is something to the "stop and smell the roses" thinking. People who don't take time to feel happy about blessings in their lives are headed for regrets and even isolation from others.

The second takeaway is that happiness serves as a reinforcement to continue whatever we are doing. If being around supportive and interesting people makes you happy, you will probably find them again. If researching a marketing concept is enjoyable, you will probably continue in that track. Happiness reinforces whatever caused it in the first place. Hopefully, what brought you happy feelings is also something healthy, valuable, and good for you as well.

The third takeaway is that people will follow happiness in you as their leader more than they will follow your unhappiness. If you are aware of and appreciative of the good going around, happiness will be contagious to those who follow you. They can always go somewhere else to work or help out, but people naturally gravitate toward the positive. Again, I'm not talking about putting on some idealistic pretense of happiness. Happy leaders are also honest, authentic, direct, and realistic. These traits all go together without conflict. In fact, happy individuals tend not to be aware that they are happy. They just are. If someone asks them, "Are you happy in what you are doing?" they may have to think about it, and then say, "I guess I am."

I have a friend who worked for many years in a high-level corporate position. She was happy there and was very successful. She got out for a while to do some other activities. However, she got an offer to jump back in at a CEO level with a new venture, and she took it. We were talking about her decision, and she said, "Once I decided to go, I called several people who had been on the old team with me, to recruit them. When I told them about the new company, they were ready to go. The old company had been such a great experience for all of us."

People will follow happiness in you as their leader more than they will follow your unhappiness.

I was reminded of the movie *Ocean's Eleven*. Danny Ocean recruits his old friends to plan a major crime, and the team comes together to execute it. My friend, as Danny, had no trouble bringing her old group back together. They had caught the *happiness bug* from her and knew that her happiness would become their happiness as well.

The fourth takeaway is that a lack of happiness can be a signal that you need to make changes. If you are miserable in your job, make whatever changes you can make to improve things. If you aren't happy as a leader, find out if there is some skill or competency or coaching that would help. This doesn't mean we are to interpret every negative feeling as a sign that something is going wrong. A tough and direct conversation between two people in a company can be very uncomfortable and not particularly happy, but it can bring great good. The point is, pay attention to unhappiness and trace it to its origin, just as you are to do with every emotion.

Having said all this, I must now warn you: *happiness is a valuable experience, but it is a miserable goal.* Take it off your goal list and replace it with something else. In its proper place, as a celebration of gratitude and an appreciation of the good, the emotion of happiness has real benefit. It is a fruit, a result of the good. But it never works out when we focus on happiness as something to accomplish. I hear this a lot from leaders: "I just want to be happy in my life." I certainly understand the desire, but happiness as your ultimate goal will lead nowhere, and even to worse than nowhere. It can lead to problems in life and leadership.

To reach your most important goals in life, you will have to experience unhappiness. What is really important in life—and in your leadership beyond reason—has to do with the values I presented in chapter 1. These values bring meaning and purpose to life. They are larger than you, they existed before you did, and they will continue long after you are gone. They make life make sense to you. And they will require diligence, conflict, heated debate, confrontation, delaying gratification, patience, failure, perseverance, and labor. No one who builds a great organization, leads people to a worthy goal, crafts a successful marriage, or launches competent kids does so without some significant measure of unhappiness along the way. But for people who undertake a life of meaning and purpose, losing some happiness along the way is a small price to pay. The eventual achievement and results bring all the happiness they need in the end.

Happiness is a valuable experience,
but it is a miserable goal.

There are two major demographics of people who are focused on happiness as their goal. They are children and addicts. They live for the pleasure of the moment. They want to feel good. They want positive things to happen to them. They avoid negatives and unhappiness. And they are unable to say no to their desires for a greater cause, reason, or purpose. For them, the only time period is the now. Their goal in life is to be happy.

Children need parents who teach them that the best way to live is to learn to love and to take responsibility for their lives. Gradually, they extend their demand for pleasure and instant happiness into meaningful goals and habits. Addicts need professionals who will support them in their struggle, give them insight and healing, and help them learn that delaying gratification and self-control will help restore the lives they lost.

Certainly, as a leader, you should appreciate happiness when it comes and model happiness for your people. But also as a leader, look for the greater themes, deep into your values, for healthy relationships, purpose, and meaning, rather than happiness.

To reach your most important goals in life,
you will have to experience unhappiness.

There is something interesting about happiness that I have noticed: *when you stop trying to find happiness, it will find you.* I don't mean this in some mysterious way. There is reality to this idea. When you focus on what is really important, and live and lead in the right way, you will experience the side benefit of happiness. It will find you in those moments of enjoyment along the way. And it will find you also when you see that a life well lived is a good life indeed.

The Focus of Passion

I was flying to a speaking engagement one day and engaged in conversation with the man sitting next to me. I asked him what he did for a living, and he said, "I'm a commercial pilot."

I said, "I hear that takes quite a bit of training."

He agreed. "It does require a lot of training—school, military service, noncommercial planes, the whole nine yards. But it's been worth it. I like my career."

Curious, I asked, "So how did you decide on flying as your career? Did you go through some sort of focusing, search, or process of elimination from other areas?"

"No," he said. "It wasn't like that at all. I just had a passion for flying. Since I was a young kid, flying is all I've wanted to do. There was no elimination because there was nothing else I even considered."

I was struck by his statement and thought about it for a long time. Here was a man who, for whatever reason, had a passion inside him that hadn't wavered for decades. A passion that motivated him to accomplish years of rigorous training toward his career goal.

Since it took me a long time, with different redirections, to finally find my own career, I felt a twinge of envy for his clear and early focus. Some people find their passion earlier in life; others take more time. But the point is that you, as a leader, have some sort of a passion. It is a good thing, and it can help you to understand what it is, and how to use it.

Desire with Direction

I define *passion* simply as "focused desire." Passion is an emotion of great clarity. It is something you feel. You can talk about passion, and you can think about passion, but deep down, you feel it. It harnesses your interest and desire for something and points them in a specific direction.

There are countless passions leaders may have, as many as there are leadership interests. Some have a vision for a web-based company. For some, it's retail. For others, it may be a communications venture, or health care. Some want a growing church. Others want to lead a happy family or a meaningful small group.

As with any emotion, passion also has a purpose and a role. Passion drives you in a specific direction so you will be unwavering and clear. It moves you to keep going, to make the sacrifices necessary, to continue the path because you are in the right place at the right time. Like happiness, passion is a positive and pleasurable emotion. However, it is much more focused and specific than happiness. You might say you are happy leading the IT department of your company. That can be a very good thing, but it can also mean that you can easily find happiness doing something else. But if you say you have a passion for leading the IT department, it means something much more on a mission and *who I am* level. It would be much more difficult to find that passion elsewhere.

Passion drives you in a specific direction so you will be unwavering and clear.

Imagine if someone says to you, "Three years ago, I had a passion for marketing. Two years ago, I fell in love with administration. Last year, I was all over accounting. And this year, I am passionate about sales." You would think that that person was either unbalanced or disingenuous, and you would probably be right. Who would want to be led by that person? Leaders with passion not only create interest, but they create security because their passion is real, dependable, and reliable. It's not a flavor-of-the-month emotion. Passion stays focused like a laser beam; it keeps you on target and tends to last for a long time in your life if it is the real thing.

When I was in high school, I was a distance runner. I wasn't very good, but I enjoyed it enough that I could say it was a passion. When I would go for a practice run alone and would become tired, I found there were four things I could do to keep myself from getting bored or going crazy. First, I would look into the distance, down the road, to see where I would end up. But that could be discouraging because the horizon took so long to change, and I couldn't see progress fast enough. Second, I would look at the road in front of me where my feet were going. That was OK for a while because I could tell I was getting somewhere. But that, too, would get tiresome as I saw just thousands of steps—left, right, left, right—and it reduced me to counting them in some obsessive way, which was no fun. The third choice was that I would think about something else in my life: my buddies, my girlfriend, my family, sports, music. But sooner or later, the physical pain of running would get in the way. The fourth option was the best for me: I would notice what was going on around me. I looked at the scenery, the road, and the houses. And I noticed my breathing, muscle movements, and the feel of the sun on my skin. When I did this, time passed faster for me, and I actually enjoyed myself.

That is what passion does for you. In your lifetime, you will spend a lot of time working with people you are leading. You may spend the time thinking only about the goal and miss the moment. You may check the hours off on a spreadsheet, and be reduced to counting steps. You may zone out and think about things you enjoy, that you would rather be doing right now, and not be present. Or passion can keep you engaged, right now, in doing something that requires hard work, but at the same time is rewarding *and provides an outcome in the future*. With passion, you gain a present and a future as well. It is the best way to go.

To clarify here, there are certainly people who are what you might call *passionate people*. Whatever they are into, they are into it 110 percent. I would describe these people as enthusiastic or intense, and that can be a very good thing. But that is not what I am describing here. Our view of passion for the purposes of this book is related to what you do, particularly as it relates to your leadership. It is a focused desire to do what you are doing as a leader.

Where Does Passion Come From?

Passion develops when we are doing what we are designed to do. In other words, there is an intersection between who you really are and what you are involved in. There are two elements here, the external and the internal. The external activity may be a job, a project, a position, a career. But that activity is a trigger that reaches deep inside, and who you really are, your real self, responds to that. You may have thoughts about it, such as *This intrigues me*, or *I want to try that some more*, or *I could be pretty good at that*. But the emotion that corresponds to those thoughts is passion. And when you feel passion, you will most likely find ways to get involved more in that activity.

In reality, then, you can't be passionate, in the sense that we are talking of, about every work or leadership context. We are not designed to be able to do everything. That's not how life works. You have certain abilities, traits, styles, and gifts. They form some niche that makes you the best fit for that area. The job is to find that niche and fit it to the activity.

Passion develops when we are doing what we are designed to do.

Once passion exists, most people know it. It's a little like falling in love, which makes sense because there is passion in that arena as well. You don't have to make yourself get involved in the work. You find yourself thinking about it, being curious about it, bringing it up in your conversations. Discipline helps passion, but discipline is not a substitute for passion.

For example, I have a friend who is highly placed in the real estate industry. At the time of this writing, real estate is going through some difficult times. And my friend has a lot of people to lead, train, and motivate. I asked him recently how it was going. He told me, "These are tough times. I have to make a lot of hard decisions every day. But I still wake up in the morning thinking about new ways to keep us moving and keep my people productive. I love being in real estate, and I love working with my team. That is what makes me tick."

Getting It

You may have identified yourself with my friend. You daydream about running your department, team, company, church, or small group.

You don't have to write on your daily to-do list, "Think about how to keep my people motivated." It's there, in your inner world. If so, and if your passion is the right fit—meaning you have the abilities and strengths—you are fortunate. Keep on track.

However, you may not have found your passion, or perhaps it's time for a new one. And if you lead, you need two passions: *the passion for something you do well and are competent in, and the passion to lead others in that arena.* There is an order to this: your own passion first, leadership second. Part of finding your own passion is beyond reason. You have to begin with yourself because if you don't love something, there is no way, over time, you will be able to lead others in it. You may be able to manage, guide, and assist them. But we cannot get people inspired, excited, and productive when we don't have the juice ourselves.

Imagine that someone came to you and said, "I'd like to be a leader." One of the questions you would probably ask would be, "So what do you do?" If the person's answer was, "Nothing in particular. I just want to lead people," you would likely not be considering how to find a place for that person. Instead, you would probably say something like this: "Learn to be really good at something, and then come back, and let's talk." Who wants to be led by someone whose only passion is leading them . . . in what?

One exception to this might be the corporate executive who has formal training and experience in leading a company. He has the capacity, from years of work, to go from leading a company in one industry to leading one in a completely different area. His passion for doing something well may be the same as his passion for leading others, which is what corporate executives do. But most corporate executives are highly multicompetent people. They have a deep understanding of finances, marketing, accounting, strategies, human resources, and the like. So even they must start with themselves and then move to leadership.

So first, begin like the pilot began. Consider what you love, what you enjoy doing, what you like because of the nature of the thing itself. It may be teaching, administration, building, computers, selling, art, music, or theology. Look not only to today but also to the past and your patterns. What, in your life history, has been a focused desire? This is not a time to think of practicalities, such as *I can't quit my day job for this* or *I'm not talented in this*. These may be important, but they are in the wrong sequence. Finding what you love to do, in your heart, must come first. Practical realities must come second.

Second, get experience. This is the external part. Talk to people, try things out, explore opportunities—however you do it, get experience in the area of your passion. The more active, frequent, and varied the experience, the more you will find that you will be able to attach to something that makes sense. The real you is waiting to be discovered, and your job is to find lots of different experiences that the real you will connect with and then trigger the passion. That is the basic formula to discovering and harnessing your passion: *look inside, and then go out and try things.*

Then do the same with leadership. Find out what you love about leadership and get the experience. People with a passion for leadership understand what drives them: seeing lives change, seeing the effects of teamwork on a project, helping people achieve what they normally couldn't, casting vision, solving problems. And they look for contexts to operate in: corporate, charity, family, personal growth, church. That part is simply a numbers game, one of gaining valuable experiences.

Obstacles to Passion

There are several speed bumps to consider if you have found it difficult to have that laserlike experience of passion. These are the ones that I see most leaders encounter, along with the steps to resolve them.

A *Dependency on Willpower*

Since leaders are often highly disciplined and structured, sometimes they try *to will* their passion. That is, they work very hard at something they think they should have passion about. They diligently study it, go to meetings, get mentors, get themselves psyched up, and sincerely try to create a passion. And that is the problem. You can't create passion or force yourself to feel it. You simply must find it. It's just the way we are made as humans.

I have a friend who was at the top of his game in the insurance industry. He owned a small company and was highly successful. By all accounts, you would have thought he had a passion for what he was doing. He did, for the insurance business in general. But he didn't have a passion for the role he was in. He worked for many years as the owner. But he didn't enjoy the burdens owners have. Finally, and against conventional wisdom, he sold the business and went to work for a large insurance firm. He is at the top of his game there also. His competency levels haven't changed. But he has a passion for his work in this context. He has a great support infrastructure and good resourcing. He decided not to continue beating his head against the reality that he had no passion for owning the business. He listened to himself, his experience, and reality, and made the right move for himself.

I mention him because usually the story of passion tends to go in the other direction: the corporate person becomes a small business owner, an artist, a musician, or a minister. But my friend's example shows that you can't pick your passion. You can only find it. So don't try to "make yourself" have passion. Look for it. Use your willpower and discipline to keep you structured in the process of discovery.

An Idealized View of Passion

There are times when a person simply doesn't have the opportunity or options to live out her passion in her career. Sometimes there are other realities that prevent one's passion from being lived out, such as a medical condition that forces a job change, a passion that can't pay the bills as well as a current job, or an economy that necessitates taking a job that's not the best fit, for a period of time.

Certainly you need to pay attention to these realities. If you've tried your best, for a long time, and have searched diligently for a job in your area of passion, and if for some legitimate reason, you can't experience passion in your current tasks, you may have to adapt and change. It's neither loving nor responsible to cause your family to struggle indefinitely while you go for your dream. If your dream has a fixed and short-term goal, like medical school or an MBA, that is different. Otherwise, your family should come first and be provided for.

This scenario often involves a limited view of passion that is highly idealistic. You believe that your job must ignite your passion. It is true that *something* should ignite your passions, but there are times when the job doesn't. So you look to other venues for that: working with kids, soup kitchens, hobbies, art, mentoring others, sports, and the like. People do that all the time, and many become accomplished leaders because they can help people in the contexts they are in.

Problems in Leaving Home Emotionally

Many leaders aren't able to access their passion because they have never finished the task of leaving home emotionally. They can't access their true self, who they really are, because it isn't accessible yet. This is one of the core issues of leadership from the inner reality. You must lead from your reality and no one else's. That journey is yours alone.

As children, we were designed to receive compassion, safety, structure, and wisdom from loving parents. During that process, we identify with them and their passions. A little girl goes to work at Mom's office and plays with the computer, pretending to be her. A boy goes to the construction site where Dad works and uses a plastic hammer on the beams. This identification helps the child to develop the skills and abilities to handle adult life. He sees that work is a large part of life, that it is normal and enjoyable, meaningful and required. It's what people do.

Many leaders aren't able to access their passion
because they have never finished the task of
leaving home emotionally.

Ultimately, the child begins to be secure enough to develop his own passions, separate from his parents'. He is occupied by an interest or hobby that his parents may not have. His parents encourage his interest, support it, and find ways to help him grow in his passion. Then, when he finally leaves home, he is equipped to discover activities that will trigger his ultimate passion of task and career.

I will always be thankful to my parents for seeing their job as equipping their four kids, rather than telling them what to do. They encouraged us to try different things, from business to health to artistic endeavors. They had no master plan for us. In fact, all four children live in four different states. We care about one another and stay in touch, but we have found our own places and passions. My mother tells me that her friends will sometimes say to her, "Isn't it sad that your kids moved so far away?" She will tell me, "They are sorry for me, but they don't understand. I really miss not seeing you all as much as I'd like, but I am so happy that you have found what you want in life."

That is how it is supposed to happen. But sometimes, unknowingly, parents discourage their children from having ideas, feelings, and passions that are separate from their own. They think the child should follow in their footsteps. Or they may think that the child should follow in some other path that they aren't on—*but it is still the parents' passion for the child, not the child's own passion.* And that is the problem. Your passion can come only from you. It can't be inherited.

The laborer will tell his child, "You should be a doctor; don't get your hands dirty like I had to." The executive will say, "Start your own business; I never had enough independence." The business owner will say, "You love people so much; be a teacher." These approaches don't open doors to passion. They close the doors.

It gets especially troublesome if the parents resist the child being a separate person in other ways. They may be loving, caring, and supportive, but only if the child is responsive, compliant, and positive with them. They treat the child's attempts to think differently, disagree, and have different interests as a lack of love and loyalty to them, and they may criticize, withdraw affection, manipulate, or become silent. The message gets through: *you are a Smith, and your passion is the Smiths' passion for you.*

So ultimately the young adult does not have a fully developed and authentic self, nor does he have access to a real passion. Instead, he follows the work path he thinks is best for him because that was what was encouraged. But over time, even though he may be very good at it, he can't own his career at his deepest level. He has not yet left home, inside his inner life.

You cannot overestimate how important leaving home and becoming your own adult is to experiencing your passion.

I have worked with many leaders who have struggled with this issue. They came in thinking they had the wrong job. Then they find out that this is a premature diagnosis. They aren't yet equipped inside to know what the "right job" is. Their passion isn't yet accessible. So they learn the process of growing up and becoming their own person. They learn to be more honest about what they think and feel, even if it isn't the family party line. They learn to honor their parents without obeying their parents. They learn to take risks and chances. And most of them, in time, finish the process, leave home successfully (again, this is internal though there are a few instances of them having to literally move out of the house!), and find both their life and their passion.

Having said this, there are also many examples of someone who follows the footsteps of a successful parent and does well with that. But usually at some point, there was a time in which that individual thought through and wrestled with the question, *Is this really me?*

You cannot overestimate how important leaving home and becoming your own adult is to experiencing your passion. Then, and only then, can you find yourself the right person in the right place at the right time.

An Inability to Tolerate Loss of Options

Sometimes people can't access their passion, even after trying lots of jobs and experiences. This is very discouraging to them. And time is not kind to these individuals. As they get older, they wonder if they will ever land on what they love, or if they are destined to keep going from one beginning point to another, over and over again. These people genuinely struggle, and it is hard for them to stay motivated and encouraged.

Often, they are highly competent and, more importantly, *multitalented* people. The multitalented part is important here. They are good with people, good with figures, good with marketing, good with art, good with computers, good with everything. And they will come to me saying, "This is what makes it so hard. I have a lot of abilities, and I enjoy a lot of things. That makes it hard to choose what to do."

That is a real problem, but most of the time, it is not *the* problem. If that were the real problem, the person would, at some point in time, trade in several good things for something better and be happy with that passion. Or she would even consider two equally good things and pick one, just to get moving on. Or she would find, after some searching, some setting in which she can do several things well (the corporate executive training I referred to earlier is a good example). But her desire to get on with life would be greater than her desire to do everything all the time.

If those solutions aren't working, I think that the *real* problem is not the gift of having multiple abilities and multiple passions; rather, it is an issue of being unable to tolerate the loss of options. Life and leadership require that you give up good things and good opportunities in order to carve the best path. It would be easy if the alternatives were horrible: do you want this low-paying dead-end job, or do you want the corner office with the windows? In that scenario, one's passion would be evident!

One aspect of character growth and maturity is the ability to lose the good, in order to gain the better. This requires that you learn invaluable skills such as commitment, self-control, patience, adaptation, risk, letting go, sadness, accepting limitations and loss, and going deeper instead of broader. It is how people succeed long term in the game of life.

One aspect of character growth and maturity is the ability to lose the good, in order to gain the better.

One of my sons, a high school senior, recently went through the process of choosing a college. For several months he researched, interviewed, and toured the campuses of several schools. He enjoyed that part of the process. But when several schools accepted him, it stopped being fun. He became overwhelmed with the choices. A school with thirty thousand students meant giving up a small, intimate setting. A school that specialized in business meant saying no to one that had great media training. His close friends were all going to different schools, so no matter where he went, he would lose those contacts. One day he told me, "I wish just one school had accepted me; that would have been so much easier." But this is how we grow up. He had to say no to the good, to say yes to, hopefully, the right.

You see this same problem among singles who are afraid of committing to a long-term relationship. As well, some people even have the *no losses* problem in deciding where to live. But don't confuse these problems with having lots of choices or lots of abilities. Begin, instead, to address how awful it feels to say no to good things, and walk away from them. Learn to tolerate that, and your passion will come easier.

As Robert Frost says:

Two roads diverged in a yellow wood,
And sorry I could not travel both
And be one traveler, long I stood
And looked down one as far as I could
To where it bent in the undergrowth.

Then took the other, as just as fair.[2]

We all have to face—with sorrow—that we will have to choose one path and say good-bye to another. But it is worth it. It is "just as fair." And it is how leaders succeed.

Perfectionism

Perfectionism is similar to the problem of losing options. When you have difficulty with accepting reality and are only OK when you or your situation is ideal, you can be paralyzed in choosing a passion. The ideal is the enemy of the real, when the ideal is a demand rather than a goal. Choosing a passion will mean choosing something that is not perfect. It will mean taking a job that has problems or marrying someone who has faults. And it will also mean going on a learning curve where you are forced to make lots of mistakes and come to terms with your own imperfections. So the perfectionist often procrastinates on committing to her passion. It is less frightening to think of herself in terms of potentials and a bright future, than it is to jump in the water and face realities about herself that are not always pleasant. The only solution is letting go of the ideal as a requirement and holding on to it as a goal. Then you can enter reality and accept what truly is, in order to succeed in a world that is real.

This is why the best leaders are never "perfectionistic." They believe in excellence and quality, and they have high standards. But they face the realities about themselves, and about those they lead, with grace and patience. No one can survive a perfectionistic leader for very long without either becoming discouraged or simply tuning out and pretending. As a leader, keep the distinction between excellence and perfection clear for those who are looking to you.

Respect Your Emotions

I hope that you can now give your emotions the respect they deserve in leadership. They need to be taken out of the stepchild role and used as unlikely allies in the process of influencing and making changes in your organization. The successful leader leads with reason *and* with feelings.

This next chapter will include emotions also, but within the context of how you relate and connect to others. Your relational world, an essential part of your subjective world, is a key to being with, understanding, inspiring, and leading others in your vision.

Chapter Four

RELATIONSHIPS

Connecting with Those You Lead

A close friend of mine, Eric Heard, a pastor who is involved in leadership development, told me a story of how his own leader, nationally known pastor, author, and radio preacher Chuck Swindoll, made a lasting impression on him that changed him forever.

Chuck was the senior pastor of the church Eric worked in, and he was Eric's immediate superior. Part of Chuck's work involves hosting and speaking at cruises for people who listen to his radio program. Eric accompanied Chuck on one of those events. During the cruise, Chuck received word that Eric's father had died suddenly back in the United States. Instead of sending someone to tell Eric, Chuck dropped everything he was doing to find Eric and tell him personally. It took Chuck more than an hour to locate Eric on the huge ship.

After Chuck told Eric that his father had died, he asked, "Do you want to talk?" Eric agreed, and they walked to the back of the ship and talked for more than an hour. Eric poured his heart out. It was an especially painful time for him because he and his dad had severe conflict that had never been reconciled—and now never would be.

Chuck said nothing while Eric talked. No wonderful quotes. No sage advice. No scriptures. He listened and allowed Eric to let go. In time, this helped him begin to regain his stability and take the next steps to move on.

This is typical of who Chuck Swindoll is as a man and as a leader. Eric had many similar experiences with him in their years together at the church, though none as profound as this one. Chuck trained Eric for a long time. They no longer work together, as both have moved on to new settings. But Eric told me that Chuck is one of the few individuals in his life that, if he were to call today, from anywhere in the world, and ask for him, Eric would get on the next plane to go there. Chuck's character, and his relationship with Eric, has marked him for life. He considers Chuck as one of the keys to the successes in his own leadership and career.

Leadership must include competency, skills, and vision, but ultimately it must also go beyond and enter the realm of relationship. It is connectedness that fuels your people to continue with your program. It is the ability to make the connection that keeps them committed to your ideas. Chuck's impact on Eric was profound, in the same way that other leaders in my life profoundly affected me. You probably can look back and remember someone who also took you under his wing for a time of development. It is relationship that glues all this together.

This does not mean, however, that you must become someone's counselor in order to connect relationally. Nor does it mean that you are to lower standards, ignore confrontation, or drive for results. Those must stay in place. It does mean, however, that you need to add relational abilities to your tool chest of skills when you seek to lead others.

The Relational Part of Your Inner Life

There is a part of your inner life that I call the *relational world*. Just as your values, thoughts, and emotions all have separate structures and functions, this part is also unique. Your relational world is the aspect of your subjective self that is concerned with people and the kind of connections you have with them. Your relational world houses your responses to the significant people who matter to you. And, as all the parts of the inner life are meant to integrate, there are values, thoughts, and feelings about these people residing there. This relational world in no way should distract you from your tasks, work, and activities. In fact, the better you understand and use your relational world in your leadership, the better your decisions, plans, and visions should operate. Again, your relational world is beyond reason. That is, it is your capacity to not only use logic and sense but also to connect and relate.

Relational Images

Relational images are mental pictures of significant people inside you. All of us possess these images. They can include people in our present, as well as people in our past. A mental image is more than an intellectual memory, though that is involved. It is somewhat three-dimensional, and more alive, in a sense. When you think about that person, you may see his face, remember something he said to you, and draw up the feelings you had for each other.

For example, you have relational images of your parents. Think for a minute of your father—if he was involved in your life. Remember how he looked at different ages over the years. Remember some of the favorite, often-repeated phrases he said that you have never forgotten.

Remember the feelings you experienced toward him. Some sports event or outing where you were with him. There may be some painful or negative parts of that image as well because our relationships with our parents are intense and complex. Your relational images contain many aspects of what happened between you and the people who have mattered most to you.

I asked you to draw up your relational image of your father not as an exercise in sentimentality, but because it points to an important tool for you to use in your leadership and your growth. And that is this: your relational images are a source of many needed elements for your life and your work. We'll go over several of the key benefits you receive from using your relational images.

Where They Come From

To use a banking analogy, relational images are like a retirement account in your mind. This account corresponds to some person who has been important to you. Over the course of the years of the relationship with that individual, you make deposits into that account. You deposit memories of events, thoughts, mental pictures, and emotions. You do it all the time without knowing it. Your mind just does it for you. The process of making those deposits is called *internalization*. You are literally "taking in" your experience of that person within you. And the account forms an integrated picture, or representation, of that person as you have known him.

We know a great deal about how we develop relational images by observing infant and child development. One of a newborn's first tasks in life is to create and internalize pictures of his parents, in order to become safe, confident, and calm. This process continues throughout our lives. Relational images continue helping and supporting us when the actual person is no longer present. Without them, we would not be able to function properly in life. Things you take for granted, such as the ability to make connections with others, to be courageous enough to take risks, to have self-confidence, and to confront problems, would not work as well if you did not have good relational images to draw on. Though you may not be aware of them, they are always operating in the background. They help you focus under pressure and create new opportunities for yourself.

You internalize anyone who is significant to you, past and present. As well, the people you are leading are currently internalizing you. As a leader, you have the responsibility of knowing that people are storing mental and emotional pictures of how you relate to and lead them.

The Value of Relational Images

There are many important and helpful aspects to having healthy relational images.

Drawing Strength and Support under Stress. When you have a conflict with someone at work or when you are under lots of pressure, you need strength and support. Sooner or later, you need some form of help that comes from the outside. Willpower, commitment, and determination can certainly help you push through difficult times, but they are often not enough when things are bad.

Relationships are the fuel you need to be calm, confident, and to keep going during tough times. Sometimes it might mean a two-minute phone call to someone, to tell him that things are difficult right now. Or it may be taking the opportunity to have lunch with someone and discuss your situation. But there are also those times when you are truly alone, and a serious problem hits. In those times, you must draw on your relational images. That is what they are for. They are meant to sustain you when you are hit hard.

I was in a small support group with Ross, a businessman who was having a problem at work. One of his direct reports apparently was after his job and was using unethical tactics to bring him down. He was spreading rumors about Ross, and, as it happens, some people believed them. Individuals were taking sides, and the conflict was coming to a destructive head in the company. In the small group, we spent a lot of time listening to Ross, encouraging him, and being there for him. There wasn't a lot of advice we could give, as he had already told us his next steps. But we wanted him to know we were on his side, whatever happened.

Ross arranged a meeting with the CEO, with his competitor there, to hash it out, face to face. Ross was not a confrontational type, so he was dreading this meeting. But he was resolute and knew it had to go this way.

The day the meeting was scheduled, I got a call from Ross late in the afternoon. I asked how it went. "Really, really tough," he said. "The guy lied through his teeth and totally blew up at me a couple of times."

"That sounds brutal," I said. "How did it end up?"

"Actually, things ended up OK. The CEO saw through his tactics and called it on my side. I think the guy is gone."

I said, "Congratulations. You hung in there."

Ross was quiet for a second, and then said, "You want to know what was weird? Right in the thick of it, when the guy was going crazy on me, and I was sitting there, having to take it, do you know what I thought of?"

"What?"

"You guys in the group. Your faces just came up on the screen in my head, while he was calling me every name in the book. I saw you being on my side, believing in me, and being my friends. I knew I wasn't all by myself. I don't know how it happened, but I'll tell you, you guys were there with me in that room, and you kept me sane during the meeting."

Ross's experience is an example of what we are all to do. Leaders encounter enormous stresses from many directions. When times are tough, access your relational images and make a withdrawal. They will see you through.

Becoming a Relationally Based Person. Warm and stable relational images help you to become a relational person. While leaders must be highly task-based, they need also to be relational in order to keep people around them. Having healthy relational images forms the belief in you that relationship is the best place to be in the world. Life is essentially about relationships, and it is empty without relationships. This is especially true with the leader.

Having healthy relational images forms
the belief in you that relationship is the
best place to be in the world.

For leaders, being with people—giving and receiving—is a primary and important focus. You draw on your relational images when you are alone, you use them to gain support and strength, and you carry on. Then, when you are around real, flesh-and-blood people in your life, you gain support and strength from them. You make even more deposits into your relational images account, as internalization occurs throughout life. There is a formula: *because the images are good for me, then relationship is good for me.* It makes us relationship-seeking people. Now you are drawing on two sources: the images and the real thing.

When I speak at leaders' conferences about successful relationships, I often talk about how leaders need not only to be givers of encouragement, but also receivers. It's been my experience that leaders aren't very good at taking in support from others. They provide it, but they end up getting drained themselves. So I will ask them who they go to for their own strength and support. And I remind them, "Your spouse and your dog aren't enough." The spouses of the leaders in the audience often come up to me afterward and say, "Thanks for saying the part about me and the dog." Spouses get drained from being the only emotional support system the leader has. You need to take undue pressure off your spouse and get a few good friends who are safe and understand you. Spend regular time with them; maybe start a weekly group. There are many ways this can happen.

If your only close friend is your spouse, you may be in jeopardy of turning him or her into your parent. And that is a bad recipe for a marriage. Sometimes I will give a leader this homework assignment: Ask your spouse, "Would you be happier if I had other close friends to talk to besides you?" See what she says. Spread out the contact, and get several people around you. That is the beginning of becoming a relationally based person. There's no place better to be than in relationship.

Having a Source of Wisdom and Guidance. The good people you have internalized, and are still internalizing, are a tremendous resource of direction and information for you. They can remind you of your values, of what is truly important, when you are tempted or don't have a good answer for a problem. That is the essence of the mentoring and coaching process. You internalize hours of wisdom from your coach. You practice the concepts you are learning. And eventually, you have done enough work with that person that, in some situation, you know what he would say to you—even if he's never said it to you. In other words, you haven't simply remembered a list of principles. You have internalized the way the person thinks and responds.

A friend of mine has had a leadership coach for a while, and their relationship has brought positive results to his work and leadership. He recently told me a story about how he is more focused and more effective with people as a result of meeting with his coach. He had to move an individual at work to another position because she wasn't working out where she was. However, he knew she wanted to stay in her current position and could be very manipulative and reactive. On top of that, he had a weakness in feeling guilty when someone resisted his decisions, so he was not looking forward to the meeting. But he and his coach were working on that issue. I knew his coach also, and I knew that though he was a kind person, he could also be very direct. He didn't suffer fools gladly.

Over time, your relational images form a part of
your own character, identity, and inner life.

After the meeting, my friend told me that the woman had been predictably tough to deal with. She had cried, claimed he was being unfair, and said she was doing her best. It really tugged at his guilt strings. He listened and reasoned, listened and reasoned. He went above and beyond the call. And he had been tempted to give in and say, "OK, I'll find another way to make it work where you are." That would have been the easy thing to do.

But while he was listening to her, he imagined his coach looking at her and saying, "I've listened to your reasons, and I have thought about it a lot. And I've made my decision. It's final. I just wanted you to know." And then he saw the coach standing up, looking at the woman until she stood up, and walking her to the door of the office, seeing her out, and shutting the door. My friend had never actually seen the coach do that; the coach didn't know the woman. But *he knew the coach.* He knew the coach was the kind of person who could and would do that. And when he thought that, my friend put his thoughts into actions. He kindly but firmly told the woman that his decision was final, stood up, and saw her out. He accomplished a task that was very difficult for him. The deposit of his coach was more than words. It was an aspect of wisdom and guidance that my friend had internalized and had been able to use.

Using your relational images does not always involve seeing or remembering someone. It's not like Obi Wan Kenobi suddenly appearing in a hologram and saying, "Use the force, Luke." Although that tends to happen early in the internalization stage, what happens over time is that the more you use your relational images, the more they transform into a part of you. That is, they are no longer what you would see the coach doing. Standing up and walking the person out becomes a normal and automatic part of what you do. Over time, your relational images form a part of your own character, identity, and inner life.

Discerning Character in Others. If you have ever hired the wrong person, trusted the wrong person, or invested in the wrong person, you know the importance of being able to discern character in people. The people you pick to spend time with are the people who will influence your life and work, for good or for bad. They can literally make you or break you. As the Bible says, "Bad company corrupts good morals,"[1] and it can end up costing you sleep, money, energy, and success.

Many of us prefer to give people a break and overlook an offense. That is just being kind, and it is how we want to be treated. However, some individuals have serious character flaws that need to be dealt with. They may be gifted and positive people, but they can have established patterns of irresponsibility, deceit, narcissism, or control that can cause damage to you, your vision, and your organization. They aren't hopeless, if they want to change, but until they want to change, they are hopeless. I have seen many people like this change permanently. However, be aware that their condition might be so severe that your group isn't the right fit for them, nor them for you. I have written about this more extensively in another book.[2]

Many leaders don't automatically know how to pick out the good guys from the bad guys. If you are not a naturally intuitive person about these kinds of things, then the best source for that skill is your relational images. These images help form a template for *good* relationships, if you have good and healthy ones. The better quality of people you have had in your life, the better your ability to pick new high-quality people. This is an invaluable ability, especially if part of what you do is hire, interview, and recommend people for placement or promotion in your organization.

You can compare and contrast new people in your life against the backdrop of the relational images in your mind. Responsible, honest, and caring people will compare well. As you talk to them, you will say to yourself, *This is familiar; it's like the good people I've known.* Or it could be that you receive a mental alert: *Something is wrong here.* You've compared that person to your relational images. In this sense, your relational images and your intuition intersect.

It's like the story of how banks train new tellers how to identify counterfeit money. For weeks, they only allow them to touch real bills. So, for an intense training time, the tellers handle thousands and thousands of dollars of authentic money. Because they have become so familiar with authentic bills, when they encounter counterfeit money, something doesn't feel right. The alert goes off in their heads because they have had so much experience with the real thing. In the same way, when you have people who are wired to be the right sorts all around your inner life, you can quickly spot those who are false.

As I mentioned earlier, during the past several years, Dr. Henry Cloud and I have conducted a weeklong training experience for leaders called the Ultimate Leadership Workshop. We have several of these every year at a Southern California retreat setting. When I teach at these workshops, I often ask the group, "Who is the last person you chose for your work or your life, who wasn't the right person? What trait about that person did you overlook, and why?" After a few seconds, a few people will groan and say something like:

- "I overlooked a bad work ethic because she stroked my ego."
- "I overlooked an inability to receive feedback because he had the right skill set."
- "I overlooked an insensitive bedside manner because she was a go-getter."
- "I overlooked deceit because everyone liked his personality."

This is where many lights come on. It's not that you chose people who had solid character and then somehow, overnight and out of the blue, became troublemakers. People with character issues usually have had them for a long time. The reality is that these leaders didn't discern bad things about these people because they wanted the good things. You cannot blame leaders for desiring a good package; that is important. But they minimized the negative, in hopes that the positive would net it out the right way. And, invariably, in the work these leaders did at the workshop, they would unpack their own relational images and find why they minimized the importance of serious flaws. A parent who was emotionally absent or cold. A long-term relationship that flattered but did not have substance. In other words, the leaders' relational images were of dysfunctional people and thus distorted their judgment. Then, as these leaders became more aware of their negative relational images, they were better equipped to connect with healthier people and form better relational images.

Giving to Those You Lead. Leadership has to do with relationship. And relationship means that you, the leader, need to be able to understand and give to those you lead. You aren't their spouse, parent, or support group. But you matter to them. You affect them. They are internalizing you. So if you want people to try their best for you, they must know that you want their best as well.

Relational images supply you with two things: the compassion to give to others and the ability to understand others. One is a motivation from the inner world. The other is a skill. Compassion is a motivation that comes out of your gratitude for what you have received. You want to return the favor, to give understanding to other people. The ability to understand comes from observing how you have been understood. If you have been valued, cared about, and trained by significant people in your life, those experiences have been deposited. They are there for you to draw on and know how to give as you have been given to.

Let's return to Eric, whose story I told at the beginning of this chapter. He is very successful in leading in his capacities. His life has transformed the lives of many people for years. He gives to those he leads. He is compassionate, and he understands. He will tell you that much of the compassion comes from his many experiences with Chuck Swindoll, as he is grateful for someone who cared enough to sit with him. And he will tell you that his ability to listen and understand those he is leading has much to do with how he was listened to.

> Relational images supply you with two
> things: the compassion to give to others
> and the ability to understand others.

Building Up Good Images

You may be realizing that you don't have the quality relational-images account you would like to have. It is common for one or several of our relational images to be unhealthy. Some of your own significant relationships may have been with people who were cold, controlling, manipulative, self-centered, critical, or even abusive. This can create distorted or nonfunctioning pictures of how relationships should work. Like the leaders in the workshop who realized why they picked the wrong people, you may have drawn upon images that didn't help you. Or you may simply reject all images, not trusting them, and go it on your own instead. In these instances, you may operate as best you can with your best judgment and your best skills. However helpful your judgment and skills are, though, they will not be enough for long-term leadership. The best answer is to build up and develop good and healthy relational images.

The principle is simple: *take in the good and forgive and grow from the bad.* You will need, today, in the present, to be intentional about finding the right people to start some new relational IRAs, so to speak. You are never too old to internalize good relational images. Look around your context and latch on to the good guys. Find a coach or mentor who has a good reputation in the community. Get involved in a small group. Seek a good therapist who understands leadership dynamics.

The more regularly you meet with the good people and the more vulnerable and open you are with them, the better the relational images. In this way, you become emotionally present—that is, you are in touch with and talk about your feelings as well as your thoughts. Open your life, your dreams, your struggles—your inner world—to the right people. Let them in so they can provide you with the good elements we've discussed: strength and support, wisdom and guidance, and all the rest.

> The principle is simple: *take in the good
> and forgive and grow from the bad.*

The negative relational images you will need to forgive. Forgiveness is a wonderful way out of prison. It lets you give up the demand for justice, allows you to be free of another person's harm, and helps you heal and move on from the past. Forgiveness is a way of outgrowing whatever happened in those tough relationships, to understand the pain, to learn the right lessons, and to be a bigger person. The combination of taking in the good and forgiving the bad will make you a fundamentally better person and leader.

Relational Abilities

The second aspect of the relational world is your relational abilities, which are highly valuable to the leader. These abilities help you effectively channel your managing, training, and problem-solving with people because you are able to work well with them. Relational abilities are skills you are able to develop. Your relational images have a large part to play with developing your abilities, as they are a foundation for them. The better related you have been to others, the better you are able to relate.

Being able to relate, especially emotionally, to those you lead, has been shown to make a significant positive difference in leadership effectiveness and outcomes. Researchers Daniel Goleman, Richard Boyatzis, and Annie McKee have used extensive research to indicate the power of being able to relate well.[3] In addition, here are some critical abilities that I have observed can go a long way to help your people maximize their own potential in the organization.

Empathy

Empathy is the ability to put your own experience on the back burner and enter the experience of another person. It is not mind reading, and it is not sympathy. It is being able to walk in that person's shoes, to see work and people and life from the other person's perspective. Far from being only valuable in understanding people's emotional pain, empathy is extremely useful in leadership settings. When you are able to empathize with those you lead, two good things happen. First, you are better able to develop and assist them because you know what's going on. Second, they are more willing for you to lead them because they experience the empathy as an indication that you understand and are there for them.

I was on the board of a charity organization, and during that time, the chairwoman invited someone new to join. She asked this man because he was good with finances, an ability the board needed to have. He came to a meeting so we could get to know one another.

It became quickly apparent that this man was extremely uncomfortable with the rest of us. He seemed very anxious, couldn't get his words out right, and corrected himself over and over. I felt really sorry for his discomfort. From what I found out afterward, the problem was that he felt intimidated by the board. He was younger than the rest of us, was fairly new in his profession, and had just relocated from another part of the country. So apparently he felt he didn't belong.

Far from being only valuable in understanding people's emotional pain, empathy is extremely useful in leadership settings.

It wasn't going well, but we were all plugging along in the meeting. Then the chairwoman inserted these words: "Bill, I am sure this is not easy for you. If I were in your position, I would be very uncomfortable too. But I want you to know that you are here because you have already proven yourself in other places. We really do respect and value what you bring to us."

It was like a spell had been lifted. Bill thanked her, and you could see his shoulders lift and his confidence return. He started relating with us like just one of the guys, and the rest of the meeting, along with the subsequent ones, went fine after that. The chairwoman had provided empathy and then respect. But the empathy had to come first before he could hear the respect.

I see leaders often confuse empathy with being positive. So they are supportive, encouraging, and hopeful. But they don't really listen to the bad news, such as discouragement, failure, or fear. Most of them think that going there with the bad news might lead those they lead into a black hole of despair, so they want to cheer their people back up to happiness. The problem is that relationships don't work that way. When you are understood and receive empathy for a bad time, it actually encourages you because you're not all alone with the bad experience. The presence of another person brings hope and cheer. When you know you aren't alone, you can bear just about anything. It is the sense of isolation that keeps a bad feeling bad.

So when a *cheery* leader doesn't empathize with his people well, he actually compounds the problem he is trying to solve. By not hearing the bad news, he is further isolating the person's struggle, and the individual feels even more alone, thinking, *Here I am, discouraged, and he wants me to look at the bright side.* The result is usually that the person feels guilty and more of a failure for not being "up" enough to please his boss, or he just disconnects from the leader and shuts down while nodding his head in some sort of external show of compliance. Neither of these are good outcomes. So don't be afraid to truly empathize. It ends up with hope.

Relational Independence

An important relational ability for leaders is to see people as separate from you and from their roles with you. Your people want to work with you, or they wouldn't be with you. But you aren't their reason for existing. They have lives, dreams, and concerns of their own. You need to be able to identify and understand that. Sometimes leaders assume everyone has the vision as strongly as they do or are as committed as they are. That can be a mistake and can undo what you are trying to accomplish with them.

The TV comedy *The Office* showcases the character of Michael Scott, who manages a paper distribution company. Michael is one of the worst managers possible. One of his typical gaffes is when he has some new idea. He walks into the common area where all of the employees are busy taking phone orders, working with accounts, and doing financial analyses. And in a loud voice, he pronounces his new idea to everyone, thinking that they should be as on fire for it as he is. Then he waits for their enthusiastic response. The camera then pans over the staff's faces. They look at him silently, waiting for him to go away so they can get back to their jobs. He is usually either disappointed in their underreaction, or he is clueless and continues on, oblivious to their disconnection from him. Michael is not aware that his people are separate from him.

An important relational ability for leaders
is to see people as separate from you
and from their roles with you.

Inspiration is as important as building commitment and shared values. But always keep in mind that before you walk in the room, people are probably thinking about their own lives and their own parts of the job. Respect that, and work with that. You want them to know that they matter more to you than simply what they can do for you. They aren't an extension of your vision. Ironically, if you convey that sort of respect, you generally receive more commitment from them, for they feel safer with you.

Relationship and Reality

As a leader, you are to provide reality for your people in the form of training, managing, guidance, structure, advice, recommendations, feedback, and confrontation. You give them the information, truths, and experiences they lack. Whether you facilitate a small group, lead a team of vice presidents, employ several workers, or run a volunteer organization, you are the provider of the realities they need in order to resource their tasks.

Successful leaders learn to provide relationship and reality at the same time. In other words, they develop the relational aspect so their people can more effectively receive and use the reality. Relationship provides the bridge over which truth can be conveyed.

In your leadership, your people will experience truth in the absence of relationship as harshness, judgment, or condemnation. They will resist and refuse it, either actively or subtly. Truth is hard to swallow if you don't feel connected with the truth teller. That is why being "for" the other person, letting them know that, and being as emotionally accessible as possible, *at the time of the reality*, is critical.

Leaders sometimes make a couple of mistakes along this line. The first is that they divide relationship and reality and then alternate them. That is, the relational times are positive, encouraging, and enjoyable— but there is no conveying of the truth. The "truth talk," then, tends to be disconnected and cold. This is generally because the leader is uncomfortable with having both relationship and reality at the same time. She may feel that she can't be direct if she is too warm; she is concerned that she will soften the feedback too much, so she withdraws and becomes businesslike and detached. It's disconcerting for people. They wonder if the leader has a split personality. The solution in these situations is generally to take a few risks and practice being both attuned and truthful at the same time, and see what happens. Most of the time, when a leader attempts to balance relationship and reality, she finds that she doesn't have to back off from the truth to still be a human, and people don't mind it.

Relationship provides the bridge over which truth can be conveyed.

The other mistake comes from a different direction. Some leaders are very empathic and can attune well to how their people are doing, but they have difficulty providing structure, direction, or feedback when it is necessary. So they end up listening, caring, and understanding but never getting to the point that there is some action step or ownership they provide for the other person. While there are times when empathy is all someone needs, as with the chairperson's comments, there are also many other times when more is needed.

Leaders who go in this direction aren't overly empathic. I don't believe it's possible to overly care about someone. Rather, they are not truthful enough. They usually perceive those they lead as more fragile than they actually are and don't want to hurt them. It is often helpful for leaders to think about how they, themselves, respond to reality. It doesn't crush or devastate them. It isn't pleasant, but it is tolerable and helpful. In that way, they are often able to keep both elements in place with those they lead.

There is a sequence to confrontation. Keep the relational aspect first and reality second. It makes the medicine go down easier. That is why, when you need to confront a problem in performance or attitude, you must make sure that the person you are leading knows you are "for" her—that is, on her side—before you proceed.

In an established relationship, where you and the person you lead know each other well, you may not need to actually say anything to make sure things are OK between you and that you value them. It's a little like a solid and safe marriage, where you are bugged by something and you just blurt out, "I just went over the credit card statement. Your spending is a problem, and I need to fix this with you!" In safe relationships, the safety is already in position, and you can go ahead and talk about the issue.

However, if it is a new hire, or a person who is unfamiliar with you, it's wise to make sure the person knows you are on her side. Say things that convey value, support, and appreciation, and really mean them, such as: "Sally, I wanted to meet with you about the quotas, but first I want you to know that I really do like you being on the team. You're a real asset to all of us. But I need to solve this . . ."

Also, there are some people who are defensive or cast blame about everything. They feel judged, persecuted, or mistreated by small corrections. That will also take some prep time. You may even need to address that attitude as an issue in itself; help the person see that it exists and that he or she needs to overcome it. I have written on how to do this in more detail elsewhere.[4]

Once you are at the point of giving the reality feedback, be clear and direct. That is a great kindness, and it is a very relational thing to do. Tell them the problem, examples of the problem, the ramifications, and what you suggest to cure it. In that way, you give them a path, something to do about it, and hope.

I once was consulting with an organization in which, after analyzing the issues, I had to give some bad news to one of its leaders. He was a competent person, but he had a pattern of being politically manipulative—that is, using people against each other in order to get some result he wanted. So he had caused some division in the organization, and it was hurting the company. It was a serious situation. His board had tried to talk to him, but he had shut them down and dismissed them as not understanding him. As a neutral consultant, it was decided maybe he would listen to me.

We met, and after the preliminary greeting and small talk, I told him that I thought he was dividing people and manipulating them. He said in an offended tone, "Let me get this straight. Are you saying that I'm being deceitful?"

I thought about how to respond. I considered saying, "That's too strong a word" or "Maybe not on purpose," or "In a way, we all do that." Then I thought, *Just do this.* And I said, "Yes." And I sat there.

He looked at me for a few seconds without saying anything. I suppressed my strong urge to fill up the silent office with explanatory words that would soften things up. I hoped that the silence would, instead, perhaps give him some room to face himself, attempting to figure me out in order to manipulate me as well.

Finally, he sighed and said simply, "You're right. I am."

A lot happened after that, but that was the turning point for him. He became more open to his manipulative tendencies and more open to feedback from others. We set up a program for him, consisting of a series of accountable relationships with people who would help and support him. It wasn't an overnight success, for the patterns were deeply entrenched. But he worked hard, and he was valuable enough to the company that they stood by him in the process. Ultimately, the process worked for him and for the organization.

This is an example of how helpful a simple and direct declaration of reality can be with those you lead. It clears the air and, as long as there is no judgment or condemnation in your stance and tone, can do the necessary surgery that provides hope for changes and, ultimately, productivity.

Motivation

Every leader is concerned about how to motivate those she leads. It's hard to imagine a leader who is not involved, at some level, in influencing others to engage in the mission, see their part, and perform at high levels in the organization. There have been countless ways devised over the years to motivate teams and groups, including financial and benefits incentives, fitting the person to the task, providing a warm environment, resourcing, setting an example, praising, giving feedback, and inspiring.

Motivation is a highly researched and studied area because of its importance in successful leadership. It is certainly a relational ability, as the better you can relate, the better you will be able to influence and motivate. Clearly, motivation involves abilities beyond reason—abilities that include relationship.

To increase motivation in your organization, create an environment for passion. When your people have a passion for what they do, it may not be the only necessary element of motivation, but it is one of the most important. People will work hard and achieve great results when they have passion for the task.

I wrote about discovering your own passion in the previous chapter. I described it as being an intersection between who you really are, the internal real self, and what you are involved in, the external context. Passion is ignited when the real self connects with the right task environment. It is how we are made.

Clearly, motivation involves abilities beyond reason—abilities that include relationship.

What works for you also works for those you lead. You can't create passion, not for yourself or for anyone else. Your job is to create the right environment for the chemistry to happen. You do this by personal research. You must spend the energy to know your people and learn which tasks intersect with their passions. It will be different for different individuals; it's not a one-style-fits-all program. But when you develop this relational ability, and get to know the insides of your people, the value and benefits are enormous.

Here is an example: a friend of mine runs a small business in the service industry. One of his hires worked in human resources. This employee was reasonably competent and handled HR issues well. There were no sparks, but there were no complaints.

My friend, however, noticed that this man seemed to be the curious type. He asked questions of the boss about how the company worked, and, more importantly, he asked questions of people in other departments. He was curious about accounting, marketing, sales, and financial services. He did his job, but you could tell he had other interests.

Finally, my friend figured out that this man was a "MacGyver," from the 1980s TV show, in which the main character could invent any sort of gadget out of string and gum. In other words, he loved doing a lot of things, and he was good at them. On top of that, he was a better problem-solver than a maintainer. My friend the boss understood this, and also knew that, at that period in the company's growth, he needed someone who could be called in interdepartmentally to handle some issue that had come up. Also, that person could give him the street view of what was going on in the company. He created the position for this man, and it worked very well. People appreciated the extra resource. The return on investment was very high for the company. And MacGyver had a genuine passion for what he did. He was good at it, he had energy for it, and he helped the organization with it.

Passion is ignited when the real self connects with the right task environment.

The MacGyver position may not last forever, as the needs of companies change over time. But the point is, always be on the alert to see what your people love, and if there is a fit somewhere that creates good results for the company, and for the person.

Freedom and Ownership

The more autonomy and personal accountability people can handle, the more they are motivated. Independence provides your people with the ability to take on ownership for their performance and for the team's productivity. You need to determine the degree of freedom for your contexts.

Some people need little hands-on management from you. They tend to not only value their autonomy, but they have earned the right to it. They are self-structured and bring in results because of their own abilities. I have a friend in the financial services industry who is in sales on a national level. He is the rainmaker for the accounts and secures them. He doesn't manage a large department. Instead, the company built a small team around him to resource him and then to follow up on the accounts after he has landed him. His boss is a relationally perceptive person and understood my friend's wiring when he came on board. Consequently, he has the sort of freedom that most people dream of. He reports to his boss regularly but not frequently. Why is this? The outcomes are there. When the results are there, provide freedom.

There are other people who also desire maximum freedom; in fact, that probably describes most people. However, they have not yet developed the ability to work without you. They need your structure, some level of accountability to you, and more detailed requirements. This is no criticism; it is how leaders deal with reality. My advice to leaders of these people is to give them a little more freedom than you are comfortable with and see what they do with it, unless it means some unacceptable risk, financially or otherwise. Let them know that it is a trial period. Either they will show, over time, that they are able to use the autonomy in productive ways, or their behavior will reveal that they need more structure from you. I think this is the best direction because then, they see the results as residing in themselves, instead of blaming them on a micromanaging boss. You want to increase to the maximum level of independence as long as it is accompanied by increased ownership.

Challenge

You also need to know how to apply challenge with those you lead. By challenge, I refer to the amount of stretching, risk, and discomfort that is required to meet high goals and visions. As the marketplace realities dictate, organizations don't stagnate—they grow or die. So challenge is an essential part of leadership. You are to figure out what the right amount of challenge will be. Whether it's in promotions, bonuses, quotas, or team goals, you are to set them up so that the challenges work for you and your people.

Challenge is stressful in its nature. It causes discomfort, but this is not necessarily a bad thing. Psychological and medical research shows that certain levels of stress are good for us: living with deadlines, having to prepare for a speech, needing to be on time to a meeting. These raise our adrenaline and cortisol hormone levels. They alert us and heighten our awareness. They require more of us than is normal, so we are able to stretch and perform at a higher level. This sort of stress, in the right dosages, increases our abilities, competence, and results. Challenge is how top athletes break world records.

As the marketplace realities dictate, organizations don't stagnate—they grow or die. So challenge is an essential part of leadership.

However, too much challenge, causing too much stress, can be debilitating. If the stress level is too high or goes on for too long, people not only become discouraged, but they can even experience physical health problems. On a management level, you have probably seen that when someone has a goal that is not a stretch, but is just impossible, the result is not good for them. Challenge helps, but once you reach the level beyond discomfort into actual inability, things begin to break down.

On the other side of the equation, too little challenge and stress is not a formula for leadership success either. Without challenge, we tend to stay in the comfort zone. People punch in, go through the routine, and punch out. That is also just human nature. If you have a stable organization with mediocre goals, you might think a no-challenge mentality might work. But who wants to lead people to mediocrity? Not only that, the no-challenge mentality doesn't work in reality because of the grow-or-die principle. As they say, organizations grow or die; there is no middle ground.

Your task is to motivate the right titration of challenge: beyond comfort, and stopping before inability and discouragement. You can do part of that task by creating a context for passion, as I discussed earlier. People who feel a passion inside don't mind challenge. In fact, they are internally driven to meet challenges. They don't need you to motivate them. They need you to provide a structure for them to push themselves toward the goal.

Another relational aspect to effective challenge is understanding and training your people's stance, or attitude, toward challenge. As a leader, you need to create a culture that sees challenge as good for everyone, and you need to make sure that challenge is seen as normal reality. It isn't a new project to try, nor a way to make people work harder. It's the way organizations are.

You have to understand how those you lead see challenge. This is a highly relational ability. People have different stances toward the stress of challenge. Some people simply see life that way in the first place, and that is a good thing. These people tend to take high ownership of their lives. They associate both their success and their failures to themselves and don't blame the outside world. They see the value of goals that stretch them and use what they have learned if they don't reach them. These individuals are your allies in challenge. Like those with passion, you really don't need to motivate these people as much as you need to create the system that helps them achieve. And when you have a person with high ownership as well as a positive stance toward challenge, clone her! She is gold.

I have a friend who is like this. He eats challenges for breakfast. He started working for an automotive parts company when he was a teenager. He stayed with the company a long time and took every challenge the owner could throw at him. He was doing inventory, sales, accounting —everything. The owner set all kinds of goals for him, seeing the type of young man my friend was. He was constantly being stretched and tested. The tasks where he didn't meet the goal the first time, he did his homework. He would think smarter and succeed the second time. He was a dream. Of course, as the years passed, this caused a major problem for the owner. My friend was likely to set up his own shop across the street. But the owner was smart enough to solve his problem by offering my friend a partnership that continues to this day, very successfully.

Some, however, will come into your leadership sphere with less enthusiasm toward challenge. They will resist it, not being comfortable with "being uncomfortable." Some will resent it and think you are pushy and domineering. Some will take it personally, as if you should be giving them perks because you like them. And some will be overwhelmed and hesitant, often due to their own life stresses or personal difficulties.

Most of the time, these people can be trained to accept and see the value of challenge. It may require conversations in which you listen and understand their resistance. But at the same time, over and over again, you let them know that this is normal, expected, and good. It's the way it is, it won't change, and you believe in them.

There will always be a percentage of people who are, for whatever reason, stuck in the desire to stay in the comfort zone. They will see all stress as a bad thing. They are stalled in that position. Certainly you should do your due diligence of working with them on taking the challenges. Some will get on track. But, after that, it's probably fruitless to spend 80 percent of your time with the 20 percent who don't want to get it. It may be best to, as the saying goes, assist them in the process of making some other organization successful.

I once had dinner with a successful man who actually told me that one of his major goals in life was to have zero stress! I had a hard time figuring out, having that stance, how he achieved what he achieved because he had done a lot. Finally, as I got to know him, I understood that he had a say-do disconnect. He wasn't living what he said. In actuality, he was a very goal-driven, challenge-based person whose talent and motivation levels made him successful. Though he talked about having zero stress, in reality, this was more of a fanciful dream of one day having nothing to do but sit in a hammock, drinking lemonade, than the reality of his day-to-day life. In general, you don't see success in people who don't live out challenge, though it always involves stress. So use your relational skills to build this ability into your people.

Performance Appraisals

As you know, you need some sort of system or process to evaluate the progress of those you lead. Whether it be a performance appraisal, an annual review, or another mechanism, this is a necessary part of formal leadership. Part of what you do involves measuring progress, evaluating goals, addressing problems, and coaching. While a great deal of performance appraisals involve objective information, your relational skills can play a large role in making this a valuable and helpful process.

First, you need to be able to *normalize the evaluative process itself.* That is, often a performance review is not seen as a necessary, positive, or integrated part of the tasks. Instead, it is sometimes approached with fear and loathing, on the evaluator's part as well as the evaluatee's. You have most likely seen things come up such as performance anxiety, fear of one's flaws being exposed, fear of criticism, anxiety about losing a friendly working relationship, shame, and even fear of losing a position. No one ever really enjoys a performance review, but it can be a more positive experience.

While a great deal of performance appraisals involve objective information, your relational skills can play a large role in making this a valuable and helpful process.

Next, *talk to the person ahead of time about the process.* Make sure the person knows when the performance review is scheduled and what it's about. The tendency is that fear and anxiety increase over time before an event such as this. However, knowing that you recognize a review can be stressful and that as the evaluator you understand his anxiety can make the person's anticipation much easier for him to bear. The result can be that the review itself is less likely to be influenced by emotion and more likely to focus on the real issues. So let your employee know you're thinking about a performance review, and ask him what he anticipates will happen and then what he thinks about it. This doesn't have to be anything emotional at all. It's just considerate listening, which can help the review go better.

During the review, it is important to *add to the reached or unreached goals, the underlying causes.* That is, hitting the numbers is great. Missing the numbers is something you want to pay attention to. But there are reasons he did or didn't hit them. If you help him see what he did or didn't do, he is much more likely to produce better results next time. It's never about the numbers *only*. Numbers exist as a signal to point to causes you can change and modify. There could be areas such as resourcing, skill set, fit, time management, discipline and structure, attitude, personal circumstances, and the like. Use your own relational abilities to dig a little, helping him to see you as a partner in his becoming successful.

I was working with an executive who was unpacking all the aspects of his work life, in order to analyze each one and see what could be improved. One of those aspects was his work relationship with his executive assistant. This is a key position for an executive, as the assistant is the glue that holds his work life together. She organizes him, monitors his projects, and represents him to the world. Though she was well-trained and highly competent, still he thought that they weren't maximizing their potential. It seemed to him that the two of them could achieve more effectiveness in their work relationship.

By this time, I had enough of an understanding of the executive, his role, and how he ticked. So I interviewed his assistant as well. She was pretty much top shelf. But as I got to understand her work relationship with him, I realized that there was an area of improvement based on their professional relationship. It had to do with his work context. The nature of his work required him to travel a good deal, both driving and flying to different locations. The nature of his work demanded more "face time" with people in different locations, so he spent as much time on the road as he did at his office.

As often happens, the executive would call his assistant while he was driving, or at airports in between flights, in order to catch up and make real-time decisions. This was fine, except that she never knew how much time she had to go over the to-do list with him. She didn't know if he had one minute or thirty. Without that knowledge, she didn't know whether to give him the overview or the details. And her anxiety caused her to get flustered and make mistakes, which was frustrating for both of them. Not wanting to add to her boss's pressures, she didn't say anything to him about it and tried to handle the anxiety herself.

It was a relatively simple matter to tell both of them that he would improve effectiveness with her if, whenever he called, he would start by saying, "I have this much time." They were both relieved and liked the idea. We then, however, went a step further into the cause. I said to him, "That's fine, but the problem is that there are most likely several more things like this that she is afraid to talk to you about, and I want you to let her know it's OK." And I said to her, "I want you to speak up about these matters; it's for his benefit." To me, they had a relational problem at the core: the assistant was afraid to speak up, and the executive, simply by being a busy person, was oblivious to her discomfort.

Use your relational perceptions so that you aren't satisfied with a symptom fix but a core fix. In that way, you solve problems and patterns on a long-term level.

Finally, it is important that you *hear the person's responses to the appraisal*. The review process goes well when everyone is on the same page on performance and goals. But it is common for the person being led to have differences, feelings, or other perspectives on what is going on. If that is not heard and understood, you run the risk of negating any value in the process. When people feel misread, yet don't feel permission to clarify what they experience, they simply tune out the leader on the inside while nodding and taking notes on the outside.

People who feel heard are more prone to go the extra mile.

Every perceptive leader has had this experience: she does the review, makes her points, and gives advice. The person she is working with seems to be tracking, but she knows something is wrong: the lights are on, but nobody's home. This is the time to use your relational skills to ask and probe: "I need to know what you think about what the review is saying." "I don't mind disagreement; in fact, it will help the process." In most cases, the other person's response will not make a significant difference in the appraisal or the steps to take. But it will make a huge difference in how cooperative the person is in following up. People who feel heard are more prone to go the extra mile.

Don't Be Blindsided

Using your relational world is part of leading beyond reason. However, it doesn't mean becoming someone's counselor instead of his leader or boss. It's about being what you were designed to be in the first place: a relationally based person. And it's about using your relational abilities to "read the landscape." This will help you to not be blindsided by the decisions and reactions of those you lead.

The leader who misses relational aspects is surprised when people become distant, resentful, or just leave. The relational leader sees the signs coming a long way away and has time to do something about them. Even more importantly, however, he is the person who—because he takes the time to connect—instills confidence, hope, and trust in people, who will then give the vision his all.

Chapter Five

....

TRANSFORMATION

Growing as a Leader

On June 15, 2006, Microsoft Corporation announced that its chairman, Bill Gates, would transition out of a day-to-day role in the company into more involvement with the Bill and Melinda Gates Foundation, a philanthropic organization that focuses on global health and education. There was intense interest in why Gates would make this move during a time of history-making success in his business and leadership. Some people theorized that he was getting out at a strategic time because competition was finally catching up with the organization. Others said the move was because his colleagues at Microsoft had become better at running things than he had. Whatever truth there is in these opinions, it seems clear, however, that there is also a consistent and real desire to become involved in the bigger picture of life. Gates wants to have an additional impact on his world, to lead in a different vein. In other words, *he is moving and directing his leadership toward another level.*

This is not at all to dismiss Gates's contributions to the world of technology and business. He has made a tremendous difference and improvement in how the world operates and works. The point is that Gates is involved in the process of changing and developing his life, work, and leadership. Though I know nothing of his private thoughts about this, it would seem that he is *transforming*. This is something that you see often in leaders over the passage of time. Another example is Bob Buford, a highly successful businessman who became interested in helping leaders find significance in life as they matured, authoring books such as *Halftime*[1] and founding Leadership Network, an organization dedicated to developing leadership around the world. Also, former president Jimmy Carter has spent many years working with Habitat for Humanity.

These people and many like them in leadership positions went through profound shifts over time. The word *transform* refers to a particular type of change in a person—a *thorough change*. The implication is that it is a change from the inside out. Think of it this way: We change a house with a paint job. We transform it by a remodel. Transformation has to do with a makeover from the deepest part of yourself, and it results in a new perspective, new ways of behaving, and revitalized values about life and leadership.

Leaders certainly do need external change, and it has great value in their organizations. But they cannot ignore internal change. Transformation is truly leadership beyond reason, for it requires much more than your thought processes and your intelligence. It literally requires your entire being, energies, and life. For example, suppose you want to inspire those you lead to greater heights of performance. You can write a good pep talk and use catchy slogans. These can be very effective, but you can also transform your stance toward them. That is, you can look deeper than their performance into what makes them tick, what drives them, and what is important to them. You can enter their world, as we have been discussing in this book. In doing so, you are transforming your approach to those you are guiding.

Transformation is truly leadership beyond reason, for it requires much more than your thought processes and your intelligence. It literally requires your entire being, energies, and life.

Inside yourself exists something that is designed and built for the purpose of transformation. It seeks to improve, grow, and evolve in all aspects of life: leadership, love, work, self-development, and purpose. It is not satisfied with the status quo. It moves and drives you to expand and be better. This part of your own personal internal world, the growing part, is the aspect of you that constantly moves you to new levels of life and leadership. The leader who pays attention to personal transformation will continue to be on the path of change and improvement. It will be a way of life, and it will transform how she leads others. She will be rooted in the present, but also looking at the future, at how she can be a different and better person.

In a way, this aspect of your inner world ties all of the other parts together: values, thoughts, emotions, and relationships. You were not designed to be static, carved in stone or finished for good. You were created to grow: to mature and hone your values, to increase the complexity of your thoughts, to develop your emotional repertoire, and to operate as a highly relational leader. Transformation, the process of developing the growing part of you, integrates all the aspects of your inner world. This is the essence of leadership beyond reason.

Transformational leadership has been a well-researched and valuable concept for some time.[2] The phrase usually refers to the type of influence that inspires others to high performance, rather than simply managing them. I am focusing in this chapter on a more specific and focused aspect of the understanding of transformation. It has to do with the personal development of the leader himself, not only a way of leading. As you grow in not just your leadership competencies, but as a person, you lead from a different place and attitude. There are several key aspects of developing this growing part of yourself.

> Transformation . . . integrates all the aspects of your inner world. This is the essence of leadership beyond reason.

Engage Intentionally in Growth

It is a benefit to a leader to become involved in the personal growth and improvement process, at some formal and structured level. That is, your internal world needs relationships and tasks in which it can be connected, strengthened, understood, guided, and even healed. It is well worth the time, and it can also prevent many small problems from becoming serious ones. There are many ways to do this, from a coaching scenario that gets "under the skin," to a mentor or guide, a small group, or professional counseling, depending on the situation and need. The point is, as a leader, you need a place you can go for yourself, not just your work. And that place translates into better leadership for you. This is the heart of growing and transforming. It is the difference between deciding to get up an hour earlier to be more time-effective and facing a problem of letting others control your time during the day so that you need to get up earlier. One is change, and one is transformation.

Notice that the growth processes I mentioned above have a common denominator: they each involve relationship with other people, either individually or in a group. Personal transformation is not something you can do alone. You simply don't possess the elements you need, within yourself, to grow in significant ways. You need acceptance and safety from others so that you can face difficult realities. You need support in order to see what is going on inside you. You need perceptive people who can help you look at your blind spots. You need feedback and information from others who understand the growth path, so that you don't take more wrong turns than you need to. And you need others who understand and identify with what growing and leadership are all about since leadership and growth require someone who "gets it." So make sure that whatever you engage in on a growth level involves safe, accepting, honest, and competent people: the kinds of people you can trust and who are like the person you want to become as well.

> Personal transformation is not
> something you can do alone.

I also need to clarify that transformation is not simply about skill building. Competencies, vision casting, people management, and strengths building are all necessary parts of leadership training and development. They are the roles you need to develop the right culture, the right people, and the right results. But I am adding to that what you need to grow and develop as a person, in your own character.

Common Growth Areas

A large part of the growth process has to do with being able to tackle underlying issues that tend to get in the way of both leadership and life. That is, much of growth is involved with seeing where we are, not yet where we need to be, and taking the necessary steps to transcend those issues. Here are some examples of very common growth matters leaders need to deal with and successfully resolve.

Self-Sufficiency

Often, part of the warp and woof of a leader's training—the tendency to be an independent person—is a problem, not a solution. You need to have a few significant relationships in your life, often unrelated to your leadership and your work, in which you can let your hair down and be vulnerable on a regular basis. Independence is a valuable attribute when it refers to one's freedom to make choices. It will hamper you when it refers to your inability to trust other people on a deep and vulnerable level.

Grow your ability to let others in and depend on them, not only for advice but simply for their presence. The leader who learns to lean on a few people can then be leaned on by many. The leader who can't lean on anyone is at risk of not reaching his potential. This is why we dealt with the importance of good relational images in the previous chapter.

Overresponsibility

The tendency to take on too many burdens is an important personal growth issue for leaders. They lean toward taking responsibility for others' choices, failures, and even well-being. You can't be a life support system for everyone. The growth process can help you learn how to clearly define yourself and your roles, so that you are doing what only you can do and letting others take ownership of their lives. I wrote previously about how to deal successfully with people who have a low level of ownership in their lives.[3]

It is a transformational experience to understand where over-responsibility comes from, how strong it can be, what it has to do with significant relationships, and how great a part guilt plays. The over-responsible leader can often, with a little work and support, learn to set the limits in the right places, deal with her fears, and move into higher levels of function and influence.

An Inability to Confront

Successful leaders confront well; that has long been established. However, when the seminars and workshops on effective confrontation don't produce the results you want, it is often because the problem is a personal growth issue. It is more of a transformational matter than a skills matter.

The process of growth can go a long way to resolve an inability to confront, so that you either learn how to confront or can make better use of the confrontation training. Often, I will find that leaders have long-standing fears of letting people down, injuring them, or having them withdraw or experiencing their anger. These fears must be dealt with to see improvement in this important ability.

Strengths and Weaknesses

There is a great deal of research on leadership strengths and weaknesses. A significant contribution of thought—represented by major voices such as Peter Drucker[4] and Marcus Buckingham and Donald Clifton[5]—says that it makes more sense to invest time and energy in developing your personal strengths and your people's strengths, rather than focusing on dealing with weaknesses. That is, you are wasting time trying to make a numbers person into a marketing person and vice versa. The research seems to clearly point to this conclusion. It seems the best direction to build on what is good and to manage what is not as good.

There is an important context issue here, though. Strengths training works only when dealing with leadership, skills, competencies, talents, and gifts. When approaching the arena of the personal—our character, growth issues, and our ability to relate—we do not have the option to *manage* weaknesses; we need to resolve them.

When approaching the arena of the personal—our character, growth issues, and our ability to relate—we do not have the option to *manage* weaknesses; we need to resolve them.

A character weakness or issue is not part of our hard wiring in the same way that our gifts and talents are. We weren't designed to be self-sufficient, overresponsible, or unable to confront. Those weaknesses come from our significant relational experiences, our backgrounds, and our own choices. So when we talk about character, we do not have to manage or accept as a fatalistic reality that we will always be this way because we have always been this way. There is always hope for change and transformation. The growth process works. It works with personal character weaknesses and issues. I have seen it work with thousands of people over the years, many of them leaders.

For example, one business leader, Brad, came for consultation, asking me to help him manage people. Brad didn't take the initiative to come see me; his boss sent him to me. The boss was concerned that Brad, though a well-trained, hard worker with a good set of ethics, simply turned people off who worked under him. He couldn't light a fire under others. They didn't *not* like him, but they didn't really like him, either, and it was affecting the culture of the organization. When we sat down, Brad said, "I don't think I'm a people person. I'm wondering if I need to move to a more technical area."

This is a reflection of the mistaken hard wiring thinking: *I'm not good with people. I'm just that way.* This is an unnecessary fatalistic stance about our character weaknesses.

As I continued to interview Brad, it became clear that he had a weakness in the area of self-sufficiency, mentioned above. He had grown up in a high-functioning, intact family of positive people. At the same time, however, his family culture had no place for need and dependency. He couldn't lean on anyone when he was lonely or afraid. Instead, the message was be strong, and go for it. It was the right message when Brad needed courage but the wrong message when he needed comfort and support. The more we looked at this, we saw that Brad looked at work and leadership as something that was supposed to be entirely self-motivating, and he had to come up with his own answers. For Brad, it was all about willpower and trying harder, not drawing on others for help.

It didn't take long for Brad to see this weakness and take the transformational steps he needed to overcome it. He found an executive support group, in which the members discussed both work issues and personal issues, and it was very helpful for him. Brad experienced the integrative reality that he could be competent, connected, and inspiring. He moved out of his self-sufficient state and began to be connected relationally. As you might imagine, this transformation then translated to his leadership. He was able to read his people and understand them, while at the same time inspiring and holding them to high standards.

The point here is that if you have a character flaw or issue, there is no reason you should surrender to it. You can make great improvements on a transformational level. Character weaknesses, as opposed to competency weaknesses or styles, are meant to be transformed.

The Leader Is a Person

My experience with leaders is that what helps you as a person almost always translates to helping you as a leader. That is a theme of this book. When you transform as a person, you engage in the personal abilities that help anyone to be a better influencer. The ability to connect, to be clear about your responsibilities, to know your values, and to deal with failure—they all improve life, family, work, and leadership. The physics of those areas are similar. They certainly aren't all that is involved, for leadership also requires many specific competencies, and the experience and training it takes to develop those competencies. But you can't lose in leadership by growing as a person.

A small business owner I know became involved in his own personal growth process, initially to improve his leadership abilities. However, as it so often happens, he not only got better in leading, but he also became a better person. His wife told me, "I want to make sure he budgets time and money for his growth for a while. He says he's better at work, but the kids and I think he's better at home too." You simply can't separate yourself as a leader from yourself as a person.

> You can't lose in leadership
> by growing as a person.

Become Self-Observant

To access the growing part of you, you also need the ability to self-observe. It is important that you acquire the habit of regularly looking at what you do, and how you do it. Psychologists call this capacity the *observing ego*, and it is a very helpful part of your mind. In self-observation, you dispassionately monitor your behaviors, words, emotions, and attitudes. It is as if you are watching yourself from a distance, as a character in a movie. Then, having observed what you are doing, you are more able to change and improve what is needed. I referred to being able to observe the way you think, for example, in chapter 2.

Self-observation often creates movement in personal growth. We engage in changing what we observe, what we know, and what we experience. Let's take a look at three keys to successful self-observation.

Seeing How You Affect Others

We are all like stones thrown into a river. Our attitude and actions have a ripple effect that impacts all those around us. This is especially true with leaders. We make a difference in the attitudes, thoughts, and values of those we lead. You must pay close attention to the effect you have on others, or you will cease to have the impact you desire. That is why the chapter on your relational world is so critical for you as a leader. The more relational you are, the better you can see your impact on others.

For example, a corporate executive I know was so committed to self-observation that he became highly attuned to the nuances of his direct reports. He once told me, "I knew I had come down too hard on Sam at the meeting. I reviewed the meeting in my mind afterward and saw myself grinding unnecessarily on him. And Sam became a little reserved, enough that I noticed he was acting differently toward me. So we talked afterward, and I was right. I hadn't motivated him; I discouraged him. I apologized, and we're OK now. But I would have missed that before I paid attention to this."

This may sound like a little thing. The direct report was a mature and experienced professional also. He would have dealt with the discouragement and moved on. He didn't need handholding. But look at the other side: by spending a couple of minutes being self-observant, the executive was able to invest a little time in a valuable person and resolve a little thing that could have become a big thing later.

Being Able to See the Negative

We wouldn't need to be self-observant if we batted a thousand. The observing ego can certainly help us celebrate our improvements, strengths, and successes, but the larger benefit is in seeing the mistakes, as in the example above. This is sometimes difficult for leaders who are under so much pressure to produce results. And many leaders tend to be highly self-critical, so the idea of looking at mistakes can be very uncomfortable. Then there are some leaders who live for the good news about themselves; they aren't aware of the negative, which is a form of narcissism.

Whatever the reason, you must be able to face and deal with your weaknesses. *The negative realities about yourself that you avoid today are the same ones that can ruin your leadership tomorrow.* You are better off the sooner you become accustomed to this reality. It will be worth it. Remember Randy, the CEO in chapter 1? He could deal with his misdemeanors but not his felonies. Have enough grace and courage to look at your felonies—your major flaws and errors—as well as your minor ones. You will then be in a position to transform yourself.

Experiencing the Present During the Present

Your ability to observe what you are doing *as you are doing it* is invaluable. The shorter the time lapse between what you do and when you notice it, the better your adjustments and self-corrections. This is also called being "in the moment." The task is not as easy as it may sound. Leaders can be so future-minded that they miss what is going on around them. I knew, for example, that a small business owner friend of mine was on his way when he said to me when I was talking to him, "Sorry, I wasn't listening just now. I was thinking about a cash flow issue I'm working with." It was a good sign that he was observing *at that time* what he was doing.

Be a self-observer. Don't let a day go by in which you haven't spent a few minutes replaying the videos of your actions with people. Notice the patterns and deal with them.

Make Time Your Ally

Growth takes time. Becoming a new and improved person is not instantaneous. It is a day-by-day process you need to adjust to, and be in for the long haul, in order to achieve the transformational results you want to see. For leaders, the growth process generally takes more time than you planned for. But as with anything else in life, you get what you pay for. If growth was quick and easy, you would have already accomplished all you needed by now. And if you have been in leadership for any significant amount of time, you are aware that building anything meaningful, whether an infrastructure, a business model, or a team, requires a diligent and time-consuming process.

Growth takes time. Becoming a new and improved person is not instantaneous.

We all have friends who shine like a comet for a few months, even years, and then crash and are on to the next big thing. They live in an instant world and expect instant results. When those don't happen, they move on. You invest in these people, financially and in energy, to your peril. The same is true with your own growing part. You can certainly make the best use of the time involved. Conversely, there is a lot you can do to slow it down, and even stop it. There are even things you can do to accelerate growth to some point. But growth has its own pace, and it is bigger than you and me. We simply have to do our part and let it happen.

This is often the most difficult aspect of growth for the leader. You don't have a lot of time; it is a resource that is quite limited. You can't increase the amount of time in your life. And you have multiple demands competing for the same slots. But there is no microwave system for personal growth.

Think about a time you broke a bone in your body. If you did not rest properly and do the exercises correctly, you could slow the growth. But if you did the rehab 100 percent right, all the way, in most cases, it would still be a matter of weeks before you were mended. You will need to be patient, not think a lot about it, and be involved in the other meaningful aspects of life and work that matter, and let it go. As you do the right things, in time, you will see the results.

The Value of Time

Why is time such a necessary part of the process of transformation? Basically, it is because the ingredients of your growth require an ordered sequence of events in order to produce the results. You need this ordered sequence to be able to let others know who you are, on a values level, a leadership level, and a personal level. You need time in order to understand and dialogue with others about the information you receive. You need time in order to think about and digest what you are learning. And you need time in order to try out new ways of relating and leading, testing them out, making mistakes, learning from them, and always moving on toward excellence. Time gives you room and space to do the best job of making the most of the ingredients and practices of personal growth.

I was having dinner recently with a friend who operates in the corporate world. He told me about his own transformation, which involved trust and took time. He said, "I have always enjoyed working with people and resourcing them to help an organization grow. But several years ago, I got some feedback that surprised me. On condition of anonymity, people said they were afraid of me. They thought I was too rigid and critical and wouldn't tolerate any mistakes. At first I fought that impression, but I began to notice there was a lot of truth to it. So I got a good coach and started digging into it. What I found was that I tend to be extremely hard on myself, to the point of harshness, and it flows downhill to those under me."

He continued, "I decided that wasn't a good thing, so I thought that if I was just more aware of it, I could curtail it and be a more reasonable boss. That helped a little, but I still had the basic tendency. That was frustrating because I didn't want to spend the rest of my career trying to keep this critical and harsh part of me muzzled. That sounded like a lot of effort. *I wanted to not be that way.* So I started working on my own critical voice inside. I learned where it came from. How it developed. And I learned a lot about forgiveness, both giving it and receiving it. I learned to accept things the way they are. And I even had some emotions about all of this.

"It didn't happen overnight. It took time to talk to people, to think through matters, and to learn to give up certain things. I had to concentrate on this personal transformation for a while. But there's no question in my mind that it was worth it. The feedback is much different nowadays."

Put the time in. It will pay you back.

Your Tasks with Time

While you can't make the process of growth an instant one, at the same time, you don't have to passively let the clock tick in your transformation. There are some critical roles you can play that will help the growth process accomplish what it should.

Be Active in the Time. Use your time wisely and well. Don't waste it, and don't expect the process of time to solve things. Set a structure for growth and keep to it. The old saying "Time heals all things" is neither helpful nor true. Time, in and of itself, never transformed anyone, any more than looking at a business plan and expecting a successful business to suddenly emerge in a year with no effort. So make sure the people, the expertise, the commitment to growth, and the resources are in place, and stay current with it. Make it a high priority. If you find that urgent matters continually get in the way, retool and start over, but don't get derailed.

Use Different Types of Time. There is more than one way to use growth time. The most common model is a meeting that is set aside on a regular schedule: weekly, biweekly, and so on. It's often quite helpful to add more involved growth times to that on a more sporadic level, such as a weekend retreat or an all-day session with a coach. These sorts of experiences can accelerate the growth process because of the intensive nature of the work. The point is not to get stuck in a rut. Nothing is worse than a transformational path that becomes boring. That is simply an oxymoron. Changeups can help keep the process of growth involving and productive.

Use Time to Measure Growth and Change. Though personal growth can't readily be measured on a daily basis, it can be measured on some basis. Sometimes benefits resulting from personal growth can be measured weekly, monthly, quarterly, or annually, depending on the task and issue. The work you put into becoming a better person should, at some point, bear fruit in your life and in your leadership. You may, for example, notice that you are more relational, more honest, clearer, more direct, and more compassionate. At the same time, there should be corollary improvements in your people and productivity.

When Time Is Your Enemy

By the same token, you may notice that significant amounts of time are passing with little or no fruit. That is important to understand also. There can be several reasons for this reality.

You Are Not Experiencing Enough Grace, Acceptance, and Empathy. It is common for leaders to find support systems that are high on accountability and low on grace. So they show up, admit failure, and promise to do better; then they show up the next time, admit failure, and promise to do better, and so on. You need people giving you what I described in the previous chapter: grace, acceptance, and empathy. That is the fuel we all need to grow and do better.

The Situation Requires More Sustained and More Frequent Effort. There are those times in which the issue takes more effort and resources than you budgeted for. This may be because it is a long-standing atti- tude or habit or because it is a knottier problem than you first thought. You may need to increase the meetings and resources. Sometimes that is the simple problem—the situation requires more help.

You Are Working on the Wrong Solution. Sometimes we get on the wrong track and go down the road a bit before we realize that the lack of results means it's time to seek another solution. For example, a man- ager I worked with wanted to be less resistant to his boss's program. He saw himself as not being a team player and wanted a better attitude. We dealt with that perspective awhile, and things didn't get better. Finally, after getting more information from others who worked for the boss, the reality emerged that the boss was a controlling and hypercritical man. Anyone who tried to please him was doomed to failure. That being understood, a new solution came out: learning to manage, deal with, and appropriately confront a difficult boss. Because the job had many other benefits the manager valued, he chose to stay on, but with better control over his exposure to his boss.

You Tend to Demand Instant Results. Leaders must charge ahead for results in their work. It's just part of wearing the leadership hat: you want to be your best and highest self yesterday. But at the same time, you need to accept the realities of time. I think the best thing you can do about this is to get involved in the job you love, the mission you believe in, the people you connect with, and the personal growth process. The more we get immersed in real life, the faster time seems to pass.

Make time your friend, not your enemy. Time well spent can make the difference between success and failure.

Spirituality

A key aspect to being a leader who grows and is transformed is to engage in the spiritual life. It may seem odd to bring the term *spiritual life* into a leadership context. However, there are some good reasons for this.

You were designed to be a spiritual being, and that matters. If you are spiritual in nature, then that fact makes a difference in your life, love, family, friendships, and leadership. Let's look first at who you are as a spiritual being, then at the task of seeking God and how all this is central to the growing leader.

Who We Are as Spiritual Beings

The word *spiritual* refers to the idea that there is another and greater reality than what you experience today in your own skin. It speaks to something and someone beyond you and bigger than you. There is a side of life that transcends normal life. It can't be seen or quantified, but it is real. This subsection will help you put a structure on this. Your spiritual side has several aspects:

Interest. At some level, you are curious, searching, or involved in the bigger picture. You find yourself wondering about God, His nature, and what He has to do with you. This interest is part of your spiritual nature. In my relationships with leaders over the years, I have seen, over and over again, that leaders often think about the spiritual part of life. It may happen over coffee after dinner, during some time of reflection, or in a period of great distress, but it is extremely common. I don't believe this interest is the result of idle speculation. Rather, I believe that this is a built-in drive to find God.

Meaning and Purpose. One of the focuses of this spiritual interest is in knowing why you are here and what you are to do. Your spiritual nature points to the fact that we are all unfinished and incomplete without God. If He is real, and is the foundation of all that exists, then life doesn't make sense without Him. Otherwise, we are just doing our best in a random and somewhat chaotic universe. Blaise Pascal described a "God-shaped vacuum in the heart of every person."[6] That vacuum is the unfinished part of all of us. This is much larger in scope than even a good and healthy set of values and activities. A leader can have many attributes that are positive and still be incomplete: a good heart, great relationships, personal integrity, talent, success, and community involvement, to name a few. But these don't finish the picture.

Only addressing the spiritual side of life will complete that, and providing the purposes for your leadership.

Your spiritual nature points to the fact that we are all unfinished and incomplete without God.

Your Relational Nature. The relational life is, at heart, based on the spiritual life. You are designed to connect at all sorts of levels. I have written a great deal in this book about the place of relationships in the successful leader. Relationships are central if you are to truly lead beyond reason. How you connect with others at deep and meaningful levels will make the difference. It's important to see that your spiritual part is also relational in nature, and it grounds your relationships. It has to do with a connection, a trust, and a love for God. That is the foundation for your own ability to connect with others. So as you seek out God in your spiritual life, you are also living out your relational capacities with others.

Given these aspects of our spiritual nature, it is a worthwhile task to seek to understand God, His purpose for you, and what He requires for you. It simply makes sense that a life that is moving along the path that God designed is a life that will be lived the best way. And that is especially true for your involvement in becoming a growing, transforming leader. So make part of your growth experience an authentic and open exploration of who God is. John Maxwell phrases it this way: "One of the key questions of my faith is, 'What good will it be for a man if he gains the whole world, yet forfeits his soul?' My leadership and my life would fall short if what I was doing didn't please God."[7]

As you seek out God in your spiritual life,
you are also living out your relational
capacities with others.

Connecting Your Spiritual Life to Transformation

There are several very real and substantive reasons why the spiritual life is worth connecting to the transformational part of the leader.

Reality. The spiritual life is not an ethereal fantasy but actually is the basis of all solid reality itself. At some level, all reality is spiritual in nature, as it was made by God. So when you engage in the growth process and learn to relate at deeper levels, work through problems with colleagues, learn to confront successfully, and know how to cast your own vision to others, all that is spiritual. To be a growing leader is to deal with spiritual realities, whether or not we recognize them as such.

I met a businessman at a leadership conference that also involved spirituality. He told me a bit about his work, in which he was quite successful. Then he said, "I spend a lot of time in these sorts of settings. I don't believe in God the way these people do, but I find them helpful."

I asked him about that, and he said, "The principles and ideas work. Regardless of where they come from, they make sense."

Here was a learning experience for me. This man, who espoused no faith interests, still valued and applied the spiritual principles of leading, relating, being honest, having goals, and being the leader he wanted to be. His story illustrates the dynamic of reality being spiritual. If it is true, and based on reality, the principle has a spiritual nature.

Cure for Attitude Issues. Being part of the big picture brings another benefit: it helps resolve two prevalent attitude issues in leaders. The first is *anxiety.* I dealt with this emotion in chapter 3, where I defined anxiety as a feeling that drives you to avoid some danger. One of the big attitude problems leaders face is the pressure of leadership itself. Leading a small group or a large company requires taking on enormous responsibility. It often entails solving large problems. It means taking risks to try new opportunities. And it takes everything you have to do a good job. This kind of responsibility can often create anxiety in a leader— that is, an urge to avoid the problems or the problem people. That is natural. However, when you can see your role as a leader in a larger picture, as someone who is being led and resourced by God, it can go a long way toward helping you reduce the fears and doubts many leaders experience. We feel less anxiety when we know it's not completely and totally up to us alone. We are being helped.

The second attitude problem that spirituality can help resolve is *narcissism.* This attitude is a sense of entitlement and "me-first" that often occurs on the leadership landscape. Unchecked, narcissism can destroy a company, a career, and a life, and the person sometimes does not even connect the dots that his destructive attitude created his losses. He blames others instead of himself and misses the learning experience entirely. However, with a sound spiritual life, a leader is often able to see himself as created, not Creator; humble, not proud; and limited, not all-powerful. He is able to see that he fails and is forgiven and given new chances, not because of his merit but because God simply gave him grace. This is a significant growth step to curing narcissism. As a successful career CEO once told me, "You know things are getting better when the next position is offered, and you take it because it's interesting and meaningful, not because it makes you feel better about yourself."

Concern for Those You Lead. If a spiritual life is sound and healthy, it will also manifest itself in how you relate to those you are managing and developing. Ultimately, spirituality is not an isolating experience, but one that seeks to replicate and multiply itself. If you are connecting to, following, and purposing after God, it is simply a next step to care for those whose careers are entrusted to you. The best leaders understand that they have been given great gifts and opportunities. In appreciation, they want to continue that process with those they lead. And that is how the wheel turns. The people you affect then develop others, who develop others, and so forth. The spiritual principle of giving to others what we have received works in both life and in leadership.

Strength to Make Leadership Sacrifices. Leadership demands your time, energy, blood, sweat, and tears. Though your leadership can be very meaningful and fulfilling for you, it can also be lonely and draining. You need a source of strength to help you make the sacrifices you need to make in order to accomplish your mission. Throughout the centuries, leaders have turned to God as their ultimate leader to help them walk the extra painful mile or to face a dangerous situation with courage. They have prayed, searched, submitted, and asked—and God has been there. The spiritual part of life is no pie-in-the-sky, positive thought life. Rather, it is a way of life that faces negative realities with support, answers, and bravery during the dark times.

Transforming Leaders

Leaders are called on to transform organizations and others. But this requires a prior transformation, the one that deals with you as a person and as an individual. As you intentionally engage in the growth process, you will reap the benefits of becoming a better person, and this cannot help but make you one who influences others to higher levels of performance. Leadership beyond reason catapults you into the transformative process and all its benefits.

CONCLUSION

A s someone who is involved in influencing others toward excellence and inspiration, you need to be the best you can be, for yourself, your mission, and those you lead. That is why leadership beyond reason is key to your efforts. The more you are involved in both the hard and the soft data, the better and more equipped you will be to execute the tasks. Your values, your emotions, your relationships, and the other aspects of your inner world can help you focus on the important, recruit and train the best people, and find and follow the greatest opportunities.

Looking inward as well as outward may be, at first, a counterintuitive process. Leaders more naturally turn to the next step, the next meeting, the next idea. But leading both with reason and beyond reason is a habit that can be learned with persistence. Here are a few recommendations to help.

Get Connected to Others Who Value the Inside World. Interacting with people who are also harnessing the power of their inner world will help you create a pattern of looking inside as normal and expected. It will form a part of your life. While ideally these people might also be leaders, so you have a higher level of identification, it is not necessary. Find people who are growing, safe, and interested in values, thought, emotions, relationships, and transformation. This creates a culture and a way of looking at life and leadership that works.

Your inner world can help you focus on the important, recruit and train the best people, and find and follow the greatest opportunities.

Become Inaccessible at Regular Times. Set aside regular times when you suspend meetings, phones, texts, and e-mails for a period and pay attention to what is going on inside you. Your inside world is not generally attention-seeking. It is designed to work for you when you seek it out. If the external distractions are too powerful, you will not be able to hear the still, small voice of your creativity, for example, or recognize an important value you have. This doesn't have to be a long time, just a few minutes. There is information and help available and waiting for you.

Become Aware of What Is Going on in the Present. Your subjective world works best in the now although, as a leader, you are also to use the lessons of the past to ensure a better future. Mike Hyatt, president and CEO of Thomas Nelson Publishers, says it this way, using what he calls a "heart check": "I ask, Where is my focus right now? Is it in the past, where I am grieving over some loss or regretting the way I handled some situation? Or is it in the future, where I am worried about something that hasn't happened yet? Either way, I am not present to what is happening now. If I sense that my heart is closed, I have a choice. I can either leave it that way or open it up."[1] If you engage in this practice, the way he describes it, it will become more a part of you. You will notice its absence when it is not there.

Tie the Work to the Outcomes. Reaching inside yourself, facing your emotions, and taking relational risks all involve effort. And leaders understand that every effort must create a benefit that moves the mission along; otherwise, they stop doing it and replace it with something else that creates a benefit. I hope you have seen the many examples in this book in which doing the tasks of leading beyond reason moves you, your people, and your organization toward the goals you are banded together to accomplish.

Ultimately, leadership beyond reason is
about life beyond reason.

Pay attention to what happens to your goals, quotas, statistics, results, profits, revenues, and all outcome measures. Using these internal parts for focusing on the right things, thinking clearly, paying attention to the emotional signals, drawing on your relational abilities, and working out a better you in your growth context, should, all things being equal, bear you better fruit. That is the hope. It is backed up by research and by reality itself.

I hope you will experience that both worlds—leadership with reason and leadership beyond reason—will help you both professionally and personally. Ultimately, leadership beyond reason is about life beyond reason. It transcends your leadership and your work and is a central part of who you are and the people you are in contact with. In that sense, to the extent that you are aware of and responsive to your interior world, you are also becoming a better and more fulfilled person.

My best to you.

NOTES

Introduction

1. Daniel Goleman, Richard E. Boyatzis, and Annie McKee, *Primal Leadership: Realizing the Power of Emotional Intelligence* (Boston: Harvard Business School Press, 2002).

Chapter One: Values *The Bedrock of Leadership*

1. Max Depree, *Leadership Is an Art* (New York: Doubleday, 2004); James O'Toole, *Leading Change: The Argument for Values-Based Leadership* (New York: Ballantine, 1996).

2. James O'Toole, *Leading Change*, 7.

3. Henry Cloud, *Integrity: The Courage to Meet the Demands of Reality* (New York: Collins, 2006).

Chapter Two: Thoughts *Leaders Think About Thinking*

1. To find out if *New Life Live!* is playing in your area of the country, go to www.newlife.com.

2. Malcolm Gladwell, *Blink: The Power of Thinking without Thinking* (New York: Little, Brown and Company, 2005); David G Myers, *Intuition: Its Powers and Perils* (New Haven, CT: Yale University Press, 2002).

3. 1 Timothy 5:22.

4. Keith Sawyer, *Explaining Creativity: The Science of Human Innovation* (New York: Oxford Press, 2006).

5. DVDs and related materials available at www.cloudtownsend.com.

6. Karen Horney, Bernard Paris, ed., *The Unknown Karen Horney* (New Haven, CT: Yale University Press, 2000), 335.

7. Henry Cloud and John Townsend, *It's Not My Fault* (Nashville: Integrity, 2007), 31–60.

8. Marcus Buckingham, *The One Thing You Need to Know* (New York: Free Press, 2005).

Chapter Three: Emotions *The Unlikely Allies in Leadership*

1. For more information on Ultimate Leadership Workshops, see www.cloudtownsend.com.

2. Robert Frost, "The Road Not Taken," 1916.

Chapter Four: Relationships *Connecting with Those You Lead*

1. 1 Corinthians 15:33.

2. Henry Cloud and John Townsend, *Safe People* (Grand Rapids: Zondervan, 1996).

3. Daniel Goleman, Richard Boyatzis, and Annie McKee, *Primal Leadership: Realizing the Power of Emotional Intelligence* (Boston: Harvard Business School Press, 2002).

4. Henry Cloud and John Townsend, *How to Have That Difficult Conversation You've Been Avoiding* (Grand Rapids: Zondervan, 2006).

Chapter Five: Transformation *Growing as a Leader*

1. Bob Buford, *Halftime* (Grand Rapids: Zondervan, 1994).

2. Bernard Bass and Ronald Riggio, *Transformational Leadership* (New Jersey: Lawrence Erlbaum Associates, 2005).

3. James Burns, *Transforming Leadership* (New York: Grove Press, 2003); John Townsend, *Who's Pushing Your Buttons?* (Nashville: Thomas Nelson, 2005).

4. Peter Drucker, *The Effective Executive* (New York: HarperCollins, 1967), 71–99.

5. Marcus Buckingham and Donald Clifton, *Now, Discover Your Strengths* (New York: The Free Press, 2001).

6. Blaise Pascal (1623–1662), *Pensées* ("Thoughts"), the French physicist's unfinished apologia for Christianity.

7. John Maxwell, *Leadership Gold* (Nashville: Thomas Nelson, 2008), 240.

Conclusion

1. Mike Hyatt, "From Where I Sit: The Importance of a Leader's Heart" blog, 20 February 2008. Available at www.michaelhyatt. com/fromwhereisit/2008/02/the-importance.html, accessed 8 September 2008.

ABOUT THE AUTHOR

Dr. John Townsend, a clinical psychologist, has been helping leaders, organizations, and individuals make changes and exceed their goals for more than two decades. Through his speaking, writing, coaching, consulting, and media work, he has brought guidance and solutions that bring people to the next level. He has written or cowritten twenty books with more than five million copies sold, including the two-million-copy bestseller *Boundaries*, *Who's Pushing Your Buttons?*, and *It's Not My Fault*.

Dr. Townsend works with leaders and organizations in a number of ways, including team and key-executive coaching, corporate consulting, training workshops, and speaking for conferences. Dr. Townsend and his family live in Southern California where he operates his own Leadership Coaching Program as well as directs the Ultimate Leadership Workshop.

To inquire about Dr. Townsend's consulting, coaching, training, or speaking, contact him at:

E-mail: info@drtownsend.com
Web: www.drtownsend.com
Tel. 949-249-2398

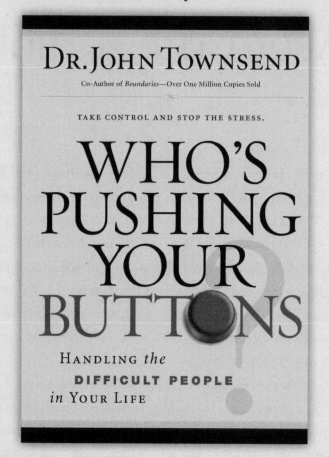
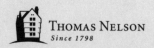